Erwin Rommel: The Life and Career

By Charles River Editors

A Bundesarchiv picture of Rommel

About Charles River Editors

Charles River Editors is a boutique digital publishing company, specializing in bringing history back to life with educational and engaging books on a wide range of topics. Keep up to date with our new and free offerings with this 5 second sign up on our weekly mailing list, and visit Our Kindle Author Page to see other recently published Kindle titles.

We make these books for you and always want to know our readers' opinions, so we encourage you to leave reviews and look forward to publishing new and exciting titles each week.

Introduction

Erwin Rommel (1891-1945)

"Be an example to your men in your duty and in private life. Never spare yourself, and let the troops see that you don't in your endurance of fatigue and privation. Always be tactful and well-mannered, and teach your subordinates to be the same. Avoid excessive sharpness or harshness of voice, which usually indicates the man who has shortcomings of his own to hide." – Erwin Rommel

One of his biographers called him "a complex man: a born leader, a brilliant soldier, a devoted husband, a proud father; intelligent, instinctive, brave, compassionate, vain, egotistical, and arrogant."[1] As that description suggests, every account of Erwin Rommel's life must address what appears to be its inherent contradictions. Fittingly, and in the same vein, he remains one of the best remembered generals of World War II and history at large, despite the fact he was on the losing side, and he was defeated at the most famous battle of his career, the decisive Battle of El Alamein.

Nonetheless, the Desert Fox has been a legend on both sides of the Atlantic for over 70 years,

---

[1] Daniel Allen Butler, *Field Marshall: The Life and Death of Erwin Rommel.* (Philadelphia: Casemate Publishers, 2015), 9.

thanks to the crucial role he played in history's deadliest conflict. Before his legendary encounters against the British and Americans in North Africa, Rommel gained much fame for his role in the invasions of Poland and France before was sent to North Africa in February 1941. In describing Rommel, the Italian officer Alessandro Predieri talked about his "two very rare and precious gifts": "The first is luck, which you will remember, Napoleon prescribed to his generals…The second gift is that of being able to keep his bearings in the midst of all the confusion of modern desert warfare. His instinct tells him immediately where a difficult situation is going to develop, and off he goes with his Kampfstaffel [Headquarters Group], which he treats like a Praetorian Guard, and puts things right, charging around like a junior officer."

With the Axis forces trying to push through Egypt towards the Suez Canal and the British Mandate of Palestine, American forces landed to their west in North Africa, which ultimately compelled Rommel to try to break through before the Allies could build up and overwhelm them with superior numbers. Given that the combined Allied forces under Bernard Montgomery already had an advantage in manpower, Montgomery also wanted to be aggressive, and the fighting would start in late October 1942 with an Allied attack. At Alamein, 195,000 troops in 11 divisions faced off against 50,000 Germans (four divisions) and 54,000 Italians (eight divisions), where they were able to use their superior numbers and weapons to defeat the Axis troops. Over the next few weeks, the Allies made steady progress and forced Rommel to conduct a fighting retreat to safety until his army linked up with another Axis army in Tunisia, but the fighting at the end of 1942 inevitably compelled all Axis forces to quit the theater, the first time since the beginning of the war that Africa was safe for the Allies. The Second Battle of El Alamein was a turning point in the two-year conflict between Allied forces and a combined German-Italian force in North Africa. While the scale of the battle paled in comparison to the battles of the Eastern Front, where the majority of German troops were concentrated, it still marked an important victory in World War II, especially from the British perspective.

After leaving North Africa, Rommel spent much of the later part of the war strengthening German defenses across the Atlantic in anticipation of an amphibious Allied landing, which would come in June 1944. But the murky role he played in the notorious July 20 plot on Adolf Hitler's life in 1944, the closest an assassination attempt got to killing the Nazi Fuhrer, would bring about the Desert Fox's untimely demise in October 1944, even as the Soviets and Western Allies were tightening the vise on Germany. Compelled to take cyanide by authorities, the Desert Fox insisted he was innocent until his dying day, and his popularity forced the Nazi government to claim his death was brought about by a heart attack or a cerebral embolism. In fact, Rommel was given an official state funeral, and Winston Churchill would go on to praise him, "He also deserves our respect because, although a loyal German soldier, he came to hate Hitler and all his works, and took part in the conspiracy to rescue Germany by displacing the maniac and tyrant. For this, he paid the forfeit of his life. In the sombre wars of modern democracy, chivalry finds no place … Still, I do not regret or retract the tribute I paid to Rommel, unfashionable though it was judged."

While there is a great division when it comes to historical opinion with respect to Rommel's merits as a general as well as the moral choices he made, both historians and the public continue to be intrigued by this man who has been dead for over 70 years. People at large continue to consider Rommel one of the greatest generals of the 20th century, an opinion shared by many of his contemporaries on both sides of World War II. For example, British General Harold Alexander hinted at both his strengths and weaknesses, commenting, "He was a tactician of the greatest ability, with a firm grasp of every detail of the employment of armour in action, and very quick to seize the fleeting opportunity and the critical turning point of a mobile battle. I felt certain doubts, however, about his strategic ability, in particular as to whether he fully understood the importance of a sound administrative plan. Happiest while controlling a mobile force directly under his own eyes he was liable to overexploit immediate success without sufficient thought for the future."

Even as historians are more skeptical about certain aspects of his career, Rommel is still widely considered "an intriguing and complex figure worthy of further analysis."[2] *Erwin Rommel: The Life and Career of the Desert Fox* examines the tumultuous life of Nazi Germany's most famous general. Along with pictures of important people, places, and events, you will learn about the Desert Fox like never before.

---

[2] Ian F. Beckett. *Rommel: A Reappraisal.* (South Yorkshire, Great Britain: Pen and Sword, 2013), 2.

Erwin Rommel: The Life and Career of the Desert Fox

About Charles River Editors

Introduction

   Chapter 1: Youth

   Chapter 2: Rommel's Career in the Aftermath of World War I

   Chapter 3: The Nazis

   Chapter 4: The Invasion of Poland

   Chapter 5: Invading France with the Seventh Panzer Division

   Chapter 6: 1941

   Chapter 7: Reinforcements

   Chapter 8: El Alamein

   Chapter 9: Northwest Europe

   Chapter 10: The July 20 Plot

   Chapter 11: The Rommel Myth

   Online Resources

   Bibliography

Free Books by Charles River Editors

Discounted Books by Charles River Editors

Chapter 1: Youth

"One must not judge everyone in the world by his qualities as a soldier: otherwise we should have no civilization." - Rommel

Erwin Rommel (full name Erwin Johannes Eugen Rommel) was born in southwest Germany's Swabian region, in 1891. As a small boy, Rommel was sickly and pale, sometimes called the "white bear" for his white hair and skin[3], but after subjecting himself to a program of physical discipline in his early teens, he strengthened considerably, and found an interest in skiing, bicycling, and playing tennis.[4]

Ironically, according to sources, he showed no predilection for a military career. Instead he attended school, showing less interest in academic pursuits than in outdoor ones, and entered the army upon graduating from the *realgymnasium* at 19.[5] Here, Rommel would have been expected to learn Latin, as the *realgymnasium* followed a strict curriculum of "Bible and Church history, with the catechism of the established Church, German (rhetoric, and composition, and literature), Latin, Greek, French, history, geography, mathematics, natural science, writing, drawing, with English and Hebrew as electives in the last two years. To this [was] added singing during the first two years, and physical culture throughout the course."[6] The strict gymnasium that Rommel attended was also an all-boys school, with high expectations for behavior, and respect for authority.

Rommel did show an early interest in engineering, one branch of the army for which he later applied but was rejected. As a boy, Rommel was interested in flight, so much so that he and a friend constructed their own glider in the days of the Wright Brothers. Rommel also purchased a motorcycle, which he disassembled and put back together without assistance. However, despite a natural interest in mechanics, the only mention of his academic talent was in math.[7] Though many of his biographers note his lack of interest and distinction in academics as a young man, his education must have served him well since Rommel was later to author two books and an abundance of personal correspondence. Indeed, he has been called "a lively and engaging writer".[8]

Rommel's upper-middle class status (his father was a teacher and his mother the daughter of a government official in Germany) allowed him to enter the army in a very competitive

---

[3] Desmond Young, *Rommel: The Desert Fox*. London: Fontana Books. 1950.
[4] Samuel W. Mitcham Jr., *Triumphant Fox: Erwin Rommel and the Rise of the Afrika Korps*. (Mechanicsburg, Pennsylvania: Stackpole Books, 1984), 9.
[5] Pier Paolo Battistelli. *Erwin Rommel: Leadership, Strategy, Conflict*. (New York: Bloomsbury Publishing, 2012). 4.
[6] Frank J. Miller, The Ancient Classics: Some Notes on Classical Training in a German Gymnasium. *The School Review*, Vol. 12, No. 1 (Jan., 1904), pp. 97-108 (The University of Chicago Press), 97.
[7] Daniel Allen Butler, 29.
[8] Ibid., 11.

environment,[9] but since his preferred areas of service were unavailable to a young man without an aristocratic background or an outstanding school record, Rommel entered the Infantry in 1910.[10] His regiment was the 124th of the Imperial Army of Wurttemberg.[11] One Rommel biographer, Daniel Allen Butler, states that Rommel quickly developed a particular dislike for "professional officers with a von in their names who seemed to regard martial prowess and skill at arms as a birthright."[12] As part of the Wurttemberg army, Rommel would have had greater exposure to Jewish soldiers, as this army followed slightly different standards of conduct, and certainly was less extreme and nationalistic than the Prussian armies of Germany's north.[13] Anti-Semitism in Germany was certainly not something that arrived with Hitler; throughout the late 19th century, writers speculated it was the Jews who were holding back German greatness, and many of Germany's most influential thinkers were exposed to an extreme form of German nationalism, mixed with a dark pessimism about the future.

An excellent work on the period, *The Politics of Cultural Despair* by Fritz Stern, gives insight into what young men in the Prussian systems were taught. Paul de Lagarde, one of Germany's most influential thinkers in this period, blamed the Jews for Germany's problems, "wrap[ping] his incredibly ferocious anti-Semitism…in a respectable cloak of nationalist idealism. With both horror and envy, he identified the Jews as a proud invincible nation whose religion had nothing to do with the Old Testament, but consisted in an unshakeable faith in its own nationalism. In other words, the Jews possessed the very unity that the Germans lacked."[14] Many late 19th century thinkers also attacked Christianity, particularly the Protestant faith with which Rommel was associated. Alaric Searles' conclusion about Rommel's early military experience is this: unlike many of his contemporaries, "he does not seem to have been exposed to especially militaristic influences, either in terms of the regions in which he grew up, the military culture of the army he joined, or the family he was born into."[15]

---

[9] Pier Paolo Battistelli, 5.
[10] Ibid., 6.
[11] Alaric Searle in *Rommel: A Reappraisal*. Ed. Ian Becket. (South Yorkshire, Great Britain: Pen and Sword, 2013), 10.
[12] Daniel Allen Butler, 19.
[13] Alaric Searle, *Rommel.*, 10.
[14] Fritz Stern, *The Politics of Cultural Despair: A Study in the Rise of the Germanic Ideology*. (Berkeley: University of California Press, 1974), 61.
[15] Ibid., 10.

Lagarde

It was during his time in Danzig in 1912 that Rommel met his future wife, Lucie. She was a sixteen-year-old ballroom dancer, and the daughter of a Polish family, in Danzig to study foreign languages. After meeting at a cadet's ball and seeing much of each other throughout that year, Lucie and Rommel likely decided to marry before his transfer to Weingarten, but as a rule, officers had to wait until the age of 25 to do so, and their marriage was delayed.[16]

In Weingarten, Rommel met a young fruit seller by the name of Walburga Stemmer. In December of 1913, she bore their daughter, Gertrude. This daughter would maintain a relationship with Rommel until the end of his life. As a member of the working class, Walburga would not have been a suitable wife for a member of the officer corps, and it is unclear whether or not Rommel ever intended to marry her. What is known is that Lucie was told of Walburga, the relationship, and the child, and she still proceeded with her marriage to Rommel in 1916. Walburga, Daniel Butler claims, would "remain an informal member of Rommel's family until her death in 1928."[17]

---

[16] Daniel Allen Butler, 31.
[17] Ibid., 33.

A wedding photo

Walburga and Gertrude

World War I began with Rommel and Lucie Mollins unofficially engaged, but taking a quick leave in a break in the battle in 1916, Rommel returned to Danzig, and the two were married on November 27th, the restrictions of officer marriage having been done away with at the start of war.[18] Much has been written of Rommel's fidelity and love for his wife, and their decades' worth of correspondence (voluminous, since Rommel attempted to write to his wife each day) seems to support the idea that the two married and remained in love. After a two-week honeymoon, Rommel returned to the fight.[19]

Butler points out that none of their correspondence makes mention of Walburga or of jealousies regarding the previous relationship, even while Walburga remained present as Gertrude's mother. In 1918 and afterward, Walburga was represented to be Rommel's cousin, and she lived in Stuttgart with the Rommel family. Few people would have questioned this, as many war-time widows with small children sought out family with which to live following the war.[20]

In fact, some biographers cast doubt the entire relationship between Walburga and Rommel.

---

[18] Ibid., 57.
[19] Ibid.
[20] Ibid., 101.

Samuel Mitcham Jr. argues that if the story were true, an accomplished and strong-willed Lucie would have refused to marry Rommel, that Rommel himself would have followed through with marrying Walburga out of a strict sense of honor, and that the very idea of Rommel's infidelity to a promise made to Lucie is out of character.[21]

Erwin Rommel's ability to lead took shape during World War I. There was no difficulty in seeing his natural ability to direct, organize, and effectively employ those under his command. His agile military mind, coupled with a keen ability to exploit an enemy's weakness, energized his troops to focus on that weakness. He entered the Great War as a platoon commander, and he had his first combat experience at Verdun on August 22, 1914.[22] Over the next six months following that decisive battle, his leadership and actions on the battlefield earned him the Iron Cross.[23]

Rommel was deployed to several locations during the war. First, he was assigned to the Western European front in France, then east to the border between Hungary and Romania, and lastly to the Italian front, where he finished the war. Following Verdun, he was assigned to a unit that specialized in mountain warfare. This unit was instrumental in several battles. In Hungary, his mountaineers persevered through two weeks of difficult, uphill fighting, and emerged victorious. Rommel proved himself in Italy in similar fashion. As a now seasoned veteran, his heroic and aggressive actions assisted the German army in annihilating the Italians.[24]

George Ridge, in his article, *The White War: Life and Death on the Italian Front 1915-1919*, explains how German tactics in Italy reinforced Rommel's combat style, and supplied him with inspiration for future battles and how to win them: "[T]he enormous Italian defeat at Caporetto--immortalized by Hemingway--was a *blitzkreig* before the concept existed--a tactic that 'punched through a barrier, then unclenched to spread its fingers.' And an ambitious young German lieutenant by the name of Erwin Rommel, commanding a company of Wuerttemberg mountaineers, was there to witness the strategy and at the same time accept a tactical opportunity of leadership and initiative 'that does not come twice in a lifetime.' At a crucial point in the battle, a Bavarian commander attempted to order a halt to Rommel's troops. In Nelsonian fashion, Rommel turned a figurative 'blind eye' to the signal and embarked on a flanking movement that bagged two fully equipped regiments of the Salerno Brigade.[25]

Rommel was in charge of 150 men at Caporetto, organized into three rifle companies and a machine gun unit, and they picked apart the Italians with lightning speed. Over a two-day span from October 25-27, 1917, Rommel led his men to capture 81 guns and 9,000 enemy soldiers, with his unit suffering only six casualties and 30 wounded.[26]

---

[21] Samuel Mitcham Jr., *The Triumphant Fox*, 11-12.
[22] Fraser, David. *Knight's Cross: A Life of Field Marshal Erwin Rommel*. (New York: HarperCollins. 1993), 25, 27-29.
[23] Ibid, 36, 43.
[24] Ibid, 53-60.
[25] George Ridge, "The White War: Life and Death on the Italian Front 1915-1919," *Military Review* 89, no. 6 (2009).
[26] Hoffmann, Karl. "Erwin Rommel, 1891-1944." *Commanders in Focus*. (London: Brassey's,2004), 15.

A picture of German troops at the battle

Two weeks later, he again outsmarted the enemy at Longarone, using a smaller force in a cross pattern of attack coming from different directions. The confusion created by Rommel's strategy led the enemy to believe they were surrounded, and eventually 10,000 Italian soldiers surrendered to Rommel.

His extraordinary achievements did not go unnoticed, and he was awarded the *Pour le Mérite* for his actions on the Italian front. In January, 1918, he was promoted to captain, and given a staff position, where he served until the end of the war in October of that same year.[27]

Chapter 2: Rommel's Career in the Aftermath of World War I

"Anybody who came under the spell of his personality turned into a real soldier. However tough the strain he seemed inexhaustible. He seemed to know just what the enemy were like and how they would probably react. His plans were often startling, instinctive, spontaneous and not infrequently obscure." - Theodor Werner, an officer who served under Rommel

After World War I, Rommel's career did not flourish in terms of advancement. In fact, it was not until 1929 that he moved out of the small southern territory of Wurttemberg to Dresden, where he eventually became the officer of cadets at the infantry training school.[28] It was also during Rommel's time in Dresden that an important political reality would develop–the rise of the NSDAP, from a myriad of socialist parties.

---

[27] Daniel Allen Butler, 71-81.
[28] Ibid., 15.

The Treaty of Versailles and the agreements made by the Weimar government meant that Germany's army would be greatly reduced. Allowed to maintain an army of only 100,000, Germany would now need far fewer officers—only 4,000 would have a status in the "troop office." Rommel, without social connections or an aristocratic background, was chosen for his distinction of service, and for having earned the *Pour le Merite*. Still, Searle says, Rommel "squeeze[ed] through the selection process."[29]

The new army, consisting of seven infantry and three cavalry units, was called the *Reichswehr*. Many of Rommel's men, as well as his peers not chosen to remain, would return home to unemployment. These men often joined the *Freikorps*, local militia groups who banded together for the defense of their towns, but they were also a growing source of extremism and racial hatred.

Little is known about Rommel's political development during the time he spent in the *Reichswehr* in Wurttemberg. *Reichswehr* members were not allowed to vote. Having pledged their loyalty to the Fatherland and to the new Republic, they were supposed to be above politics. Searle, however, is careful to point out that not voting was not equivalent to having no political opinions, and what is known about the culture of the *Reichswehr* officer corps can be drawn from the man who led it, Hans von Seeckt, its commanding officer.[30] For von Seeckt, it was necessary that the 4,000 men he was limited to in his officer corps be the right kind of men. Certainly, an army of 100,000 could not defend Germany, but the few thousand officers that von Seeckt was preparing would need to be ready to command a larger army made up of the German people, particularly the young *Freikorps*, should the occasion arise. Young calls the officers corps "a hard core of professionals with which [von Seeckt] could lay the foundations of the army of the future. They were the reinforcement, the steel frame, on to which the concrete of conscripts could quickly be poured, if and when it became possible to reintroduce conscription, as was done by Hitler in March, 1935."[31]

---

[29] Ibid., 13.
[30] Ibid., 96.
[31] Desmond Young, 50.

Hans von Seeckt

The Weimar government was hated by both the right and the left—those who wished for a return to an imperial Germany, and those who desired a new and more radical government style.[32] Von Seeckt, knowing the instability of the government and concerned with long-term goals for German recovery, made clear that his officers, who would commit to 25 years upon joining the *Reichswehr* officer corps, were "an example for all German men—indeed, for all German people—by their conduct, deportment speech, and above all, their character."[33] Von Seeckt rallied his men, banned from training with real weapons and encumbered by restrictions on the number of enlisted, with a vision for future conflict: "If fate once again calls the German people to arms, and who can doubt that day will come, then officers should not have to call on a nation of weaklings, but of strong men ready to take up familiar and trusted weapons. The form these weapons take is not important as long as they are wielded by hands of steel and hearts of iron. So let us do our utmost to ensure that on that future day there is no lack of such hearts and hands. Let us strive tirelessly to strengthen our own bodies and minds and those of our fellow Germans...It is the duty of every member of the general staff to make the Reichswehr not only a reliable pillar of the state, but also a school for the leaders of the nation. Beyond the army itself, every officer will sow the seed of manly attitudes throughout the population."[34]

---

[32] Alaric Searle, 15.
[33] Daniel Allen Butler, 97.
[34] Wolfram Wette, *The Wehrmacht*. (Boston: Harvard University Press, 2009), 145.

The broad education that Rommel had received would put him in good standing with von Seeckt's expectations for his general staff. Von Seeckt prided himself on his manners, his writing, and his knowledge of history and culture, as well as pursuit of military technology.[35] A discussion of von Seeckt's vision, however, should not lead one to the belief that the men of the German *Reichswehr* were all of one mind. Instead, many were disillusioned, angry, humiliated, and living in poor conditions. This was especially true of the navy sailors under Rommel's charge. Since the Versailles Treaty had forbidden the Germans from maintaining a navy, these sailors were now army men. Butler records a story in which Rommel, derided by his men for wearing his World War I medals, replied by telling them of his prayers for them during his evenings at the front: "My prayers were heard, because here you are." As Rommel would later write in his *Infantry Attacks*, "Winning the men's confidence requires much of a commander. He must exercise care and caution, look after his men, live under the same hardships, and—above all—apply self-discipline. But once he has their confidence, his men will follow him through hell and high water."[36] This was certainly true in Rommel's life, and the former sailors gave Rommel no more trouble.

Daniel Butler contends that it was von Seeckt's influence that may have kept Rommel from aligning himself to a political party, resulting in the "perfect non-political Reichswehr officer."[37] Offering a counter-argument to Searle's assertion that Rommel was likely influenced by the rise of national socialist parties in the 1920s and 30s, Butler claims that before Hitler rose to power legally in 1933, "the Nazis were fundamentally irrelevant to him, both personally and professionally."[38]

At the same time, there was a dark side to von Seeckt's leadership. The head of the *Reichswehr's* disdain for politics extended to the republic which he was supposed to be defending. Instead, von Seeckt desired the restoration of German pride, something he believed could only be accomplished through rearmament. The Versailles Treaty (and the Weimar government's at least public adherence to it) was, to von Seeckt, an embarrassment and a hurdle to be overcome. In 1921, he created the *R Sondergruppe*, a secret organization within the *Reichswehr* whose purpose was to acquire help from the Soviet Union to evade the arms limitations of Versailles. The R-group sought modern weapons technology, including planes, tanks, and poison gas, that the army could access for training and in the future.[39] The result was well over $200 million (adjusted for inflation) being secretly funneled to the Soviets, at a time when the German people were suffering from horrible inflation, unemployment, and in some cases malnutrition or starvation. Butler describes the top leadership of the *Reichswehr* as discounting the failing and increasingly disregarded Weimar government, and seeing the

---

[35] Daniel Allen Butler, 100.
[36] Erwin Rommel, *Infantry Attacks*. (Bamsley: South Yorkshire: Greenhill Books, 1990).
[37] Daniel Allen Butler, 111.
[38] Ibid.
[39] Ibid., 108.

Reichswehr as a force loyal to the German people, rather than to any one government.[40]

Meanwhile, in Dresden, Rommel put to use his experience from World War I, instructing junior officers in infantry tactics. He emerged as a natural teacher, using his drawing talent to illustrate his lectures.[41] In all, Rommel spent four years as an instructor of cadets, and later recalled, "I was never happier than when working with young soldiers."[42]

Furthermore, Rommel wrote what would become a best-selling book, *Infantry Attacks*. Based on his World War I experiences, it has been called "an excellent little manual of infantry tactics."[43] Rommel's book, created as he taught at the infantry training school, provided specific accounts of World War I campaigns, as well as offering strategic advice: "It is my experience that bold decisions give the best promise of success. But one must differentiate between [strategic] and tactical boldness and a military gamble. A bold operation is one in which success is not a certainty but which in case of failure leaves one with sufficient forces in hand to cope with whatever situation may arise. A gamble, on the other hand, is an operation which can lead either to victory or to the complete destruction of one's force. Situations can arise where even gamble may be justified--as, for instance, when in the normal course of events defeat is merely a matter of time, when the gaining of time is therefore pointless and the only chance lies in an operation of great risk." *Infantry Attacks* became a training manual for the Swiss, and decades later, it was still being used to instruct desert forces in the Gulf Wars.

In 1933, Rommel was transferred from his position at the cadet school to a mountain battalion known as *Jager*, meaning Hunter battalion, and upon his arrival, he found himself having to earn the respect of the men he would command. The battalion was untrained and had been allowed to fall into a state of apathy. After more than proving his own physical skills in climbing to the top of a mountain by rope and skiing down four different times after a challenge, he began to institute a new training regimen. Men in Rommel's unit were expected to run two miles a day at minimum, to perform at his own high standard of marksmanship, and - a skill previously and ironically missing - to hunt.[44] After two years, Rommel was again promoted, this time to the rank of Lieutenant Colonel.

Chapter 3: The Nazis

"The art of concentrating strength at one point, forcing a breakthrough, rolling up and securing the flanks on either side, and then penetrating like lightning, before the enemy has time to react, deep into his rear." – Rommel

Though Rommel never joined the Nazi Party, he obviously worked closely with Nazi leaders

---

[40] Ibid.
[41] Ibid., 106.
[42] Ibid.
[43] Desmond Young, 54.
[44] Daniel Allen Butler, 114.

from 1935 until the end of his life. It is understandable that many who find themselves intrigued by Rommel's military accomplishments and reputation as a man of honor, seek to know just how closely Rommel aligned himself with Nazi values. Is it possible he was simply ignorant of Nazi rhetoric? Was he completely apolitical? Was he naive?

A brief description of post-war German politics is necessary to develop a full picture of Rommel's leanings. With World War I over and the German armies defeated, the Allies pursued several goals in negotiating a treaty. The French, and to a lesser degree the British, demanded payment, and a guarantee that Germany be reduced industrially and militarily so as not to become a threat to European security again. The infamous "blame clause" or "war guilt clause" contained in the Treaty of Versailles forced Germany to take responsibility for the start of the war. It also meant the Germans must pay astronomical, and in retrospect, unreasonable, reparations to the Allied powers.

Many of the German people believed that their new Weimar Republic was an embarrassment. Some longed for the days of the imperial German government and a strong Kaiser. Young people, however, tended to fall into one of two camps, the parties of the left and right. Those on the left called for greater government initiatives to aid the German people in their recovery from the war. The left included soft-socialists who desired increased social programs, unemployment benefits, and government jobs, to communists who sought to topple the Weimar government, and usher in a utopia of government ownership.

On the right were those mostly concerned with German pride and honor. They saw the Weimar governments as groveling and weak leaders who either could not or would not do anything to restore Germany to her former greatness. Many of these parties were national socialist parties, meaning that they called for government ownership of large corporations but emphasized nationalism rather than the international communist brotherhood of the left. The right also called for law and order in the increasing havoc of 1920s and '30s Germany. Promising the people security and protection from crime, the parties on the right used their influence on young people, espeially those who were unemployed and with little to do, to form vigilante-type organizations.

There is more evidence to support a somewhat apolitical Rommel than to align him with any one party before Hitler's rise to power. Butler describes Rommel as "a little to the left of center" in the political spectrum of Weimar Germany. With that in mind, just when did Rommel become associated with the Nazis? This is still a highly debated question amongst historians, but some timeline of events is possible to reconstruct.

On June 30, 1934, the Night of the Long Knives, Hitler's attack on his former allies in the SA took place. The SA was a militia organization that had helped to propel National Socialist parties to power. Made up of former soldiers as well as unemployed youth and petty criminals, it had grown, along with Germany's discontent, to over one million men. For a newly empowered leader, but one without a mandate, the SA was a threat. In 1934, Hitler used his personal force, the SS, to systematically arrest SA members, murdering over 85 of them. The Reischwehr hated the SA for its violence and thuggery, as well as for its competition for the German people's loyalty and regard. The head of the SA, Ernst Rohm, who was killed during the Night of the Long Knives, desired to bring the *Reichswehr* under SA control, something the army officers simply could not bear.

Hitler and Rohm

What Rommel thought of the attack on the SA is difficult to determine. Samuel Mitcham reports that Rommel was said to have supported the actions against the SA as necessary to avoid their taking over the German government completely, while contrasting this with a comment made to a peer that the incident was a missed opportunity to be rid of "Hitler and his whole gang."[45] Desmond Young states that Rommel "was not horrified when he heard that Rohm and the rest had been liquidated on the Night of the Long Knives, June 30th, 1934. He believed the story that they had been plotting to overthrow Hitler and seize power for themselves, and thought they had gotten their just deserts." [46]

Rommel may have agreed with the need for the SA to be dealt with, but perhaps not with the severity of the attack. He reportedly told an adjutant, "The Fuhrer didn't have to do that. He doesn't realize how powerful he is, otherwise he could have exercised his strength in a more powerful and generous way."[47]

Butler points out here that Rommel's comment reveals an "essential naivety" about Hitler's aims, but this is difficult to reconcile with Hitler's speech justifying the action: "It was in this hour I was responsible for the fate of the German people, and thereby I became the supreme justiciar of the German people!... I gave the order to shoot those who were the ringleaders in this treason, and I further gave the order to burn out down to the raw flesh the ulcers of this poisoning of the wells in our domestic life and of the poisoning of the outside world. And I further ordered that if any of the mutineers should attempt to resist arrest, they were immediately to be struck down with armed force. The nation must know that its existence --and that is guaranteed through its internal order and security--can be threatened by no one with impunity! And everyone must know for all future time that if he raises his hand to strike the state, then certain death is his lot."

Young, one of Rommel's most sympathetic biographers, portrays Rommel as ranging from neutral to politics in general, citing von Seeckt's standard for his officers, to slightly critical in a comment he made to his wife concerning Hitler's associates. He writes, "[Rommel] had been brought up in a non-political society in a small German provincial town; he had been educated as a soldier; he had left for the wars when he was not yet twenty-three. He had been only too glad, when he returned, to escape from the dissensions of post-war Germany to the one world in which he felt at home. Coffee-housing was not among his amusements, he read little and was not in the least politically minded. The only comment which Frau Rommel remembers him making in the early days was that they 'seemed to be a set of scallywags' and that it was a pity that Hitler surrounded himself with such people."[48]

---

[45] Samuel Mitcham Jr., 23.
[46] Desmond Young, 56.
[47] Daniel Allen Butler, 122.
[48] Ibid., 55.

During a Thanksgiving celebration, *Reichsbaurentag*,[49] Rommel met Hitler for the first time. Rommel was informed that his Jaegers would parade by the Fuhrer, but that his men would be divided from Hitler by a line of SS guards. Rommel informed the representative of the SS that this would be unacceptable as an offense to his men, since the SS "guard" would imply that Hitler needed protection from Germany's own troops. After a quickly arranged meeting with Himmler and propaganda minister Joseph Goebbels during which he was reassured that no SS guard line would be present and that the idea had been a mistake on the part of an SS member, Rommel agreed to participate. He met Hitler and was complimented on the appearance of his Jaeger battalion.[50]

Hitler with Rommel to his left in 1934

---

[49] Nicholas Varangis, "Rommel's Ghost Division." *Warfare History Network: WWII.* June 1, 2016.
[50] Ibid., 56-57.

Goebbels

In 1937, Rommel was appointed to the position of "first liaison officer to Hitler Youth leadership."[51] He would, however, hold this position only for a short time, and there is controversy over the reason for Rommel's departure from the Hitler Youth position in 1938. Rommel's sympathetic biographers argue there was conflict between Rommel and the head of Hitler Youth, Baldur von Schirach, the issue being Rommel's objection to Schirach's style, which he deemed too militaristic. Ian Beckett, in his *Rommel: A Reappraisal*, seeks to dismiss the idea that Rommel had some sort of issue with the Nazis or their leadership, claiming, instead,

---

[51] Michael H. Kater, *Hitler Youth* (Cambridge, MA: Harvard University Press, 2004), 29.

that Schirach objected to Rommel's insistence the Hitler Youth be taken over by the *Wehrmacht*.[52] While Beckett discusses a private remark that was supposed to have been made by Schirach to the effect that "Rommel could not be regarded as a Nazi,"[53] he also cautions against reading too much into what was likely a conflict over power, not ideology.[54]

Schirach (right) with Hitler, Bormann and Göring at the Obersalzberg

Beckett points out that Rommel's position in late 1938-1939 as commander of an Austrian War academy would not likely have been awarded to someone whose loyalty to Nazi ideology was in question. He accuses Rommel's sympathetic biographers of whitewashing his links to the Nazi Party, or at the very least, of failing to reveal all that the historical record shows of Rommel's contact with Nazi party members.[55] It was here, in Austria that Rommel wrote to his wife about a speech Hitler delivered in December of 1938: "The Fuhrer spoke yesterday: the soldier today must be political because he must always be ready to go into action for the new politics. The German *Wehrmacht* is the sword of the new German worldview."[56] For Beckett, this is an unmistakable "sign of [Rommel's] drift toward uncritical support of Nazi policies."[57]

---

[52] Ian F. Beckett, 20.
[53] Ibid., 21.
[54] Ibid.
[55] Ibid., 22.
[56] Ibid.
[57] Ibid.

Still, Desmond Young asserts that it was the Nazi propaganda efforts led by Joseph Goebbels, not the actual story of Rommel, that attempted to paint him falsely as the son of a factory worker, a member of the *Freikorps*, a Stormtrooper, and a personal friend to Hitler.[58] These "facts" appeared in an article in *Das Reich*, and according to Young, Rommel set out to try to discover who had supplied the incorrect information, only to hear that "it could only do good by making him a more familiar and sympathetic figure to the foreign war correspondents. Perhaps…it would have been a good thing, from the propaganda point of view, if the statements, though admittedly incorrect, had, in fact, been true."[59]

In October 1938, after reading *Infantry Attacks*, Hitler selected Rommel to be his escort during his march into the Sudetenland. In this position, Rommel had charge of over 300 men and received a promotion to colonel after completing his service to the Fuhrer. As colonel, he would take up a new teaching position at the war school south of Vienna.[60] When he was called back to guard duty for Hitler after the full German invasion of Czechoslovakia in March of 1939, Rommel seemed to believe his fortunes were improving and described for his wife how he "persuaded [Hitler] to drive on [in face of a missing SS escort] under my personal protection. He put himself in my hands." An impressed Rommel then ventured a question: "Isn't it wonderful that we have this man?"[61]

Chapter 4: The Invasion of Poland

"Rommel was a military phenomenon that can occur only at rare intervals; men of such bravery and daring survive only with exceptional fortune. He was as brave on the battlefield as Ney, with much better brains; as dashing as Murat, with better balance; as cool and as quick a tactician as Wellington." - Field Marshal Archibald Wavell

Having found success in his taking of Czechoslovakia and growing more unafraid of the French and British with each passing day, by August of 1939, Hitler was ready to invade Poland. For this, Hitler required guards for his mobile headquarters, and Rommel was once again called upon for the job. The now newly promoted Major-General would lead the same men he had in the Sudetenland.[62] Both Rommel and Lucie believed, as did many Germans, that the Danzig Corridor created by Versailles had been a travesty, and rightly belonged to Germany. Even Desmond Young admits, "It would be idle to pretend that Rommel had any qualms of conscience over invading Poland."[63]

With a bunch of false flags completed to give Germany a pretext for the invasion, thousands of Panzer I, II, and III tanks, accompanied by trucks, halftracks, and motorcycles, rolled forward

---

[58] Desmond Young, 25-27
[59] Ibid., 27.
[60] Terry Brighton, *Patton, Montgomery, and Rommel: Masters of War.* (New York: Crown Publishers, 2008), 61.
[61] Ibid., 61.
[62] Ibid., 63.
[63] Desmond Young, 66.

towards the Polish border in the pre-dawn darkness of September 1st, 1939. Hitler had launched "Case White" at last, and with it, the start of World War II, which would ultimately lead to some 60 million deaths, including his own, practically all other high Nazi officials, and also Rommel's.

Although the campaign in Poland is typically overlooked, especially in comparison to some of the incredibly large and violent campaigns in subsequent years, it was instrumental in providing the Nazi forces with experience they would use across Europe and in Russia. After all, it was in Poland that the Wehrmacht saw action for the first time, conducting what was not only an invasion but also a trial run of its new equipment and tactics. The Polish invasion proved invaluable in providing the German high command with a low-risk, high-value live fire exercise for their newly minted war machine, while the actual combat experience highlighted the remaining flaws in the system. During the campaign, the Germans honed tactics and weapon systems for the massive struggle with the Soviets, British, and United States that loomed on the horizon.

The Wehrmacht adopted a very bold, large-scale strategy, using two huge encircling movements to chop Polish territory into thirds. Army Group North, starting from East Prussia and northern Germany, launched two main thrusts southeast, while Army Group South, based in Germany and Czechoslovakia, launched two thrusts northwest. The Germans intended these pincer movements to converge at Warsaw and Brest-Litovsk, thereby cutting off and encircling vast numbers of Polish soldiers, who would be compelled to surrender or be annihilated.

For their part, the Poles predicated their strategy on fighting a delaying action in the west, accompanied by a slow withdrawal eastward. The Poles still believed the Soviets would not attack them; in fact, a few Polish leaders, more sanguine than the rest, thought the Russians might send aid to them to help expel the Germans. They also trusted their new alliance with the British and French to provide speedy relief. Both of these Polish hopes proved hollow.

One rather unexpected presence at the front was Adolf Hitler himself. Hitler personally crossed into Poland on September 4, 1939, with his train under the watchful eye of Rommel himself.[64] Not yet weakened by illness, drugs, and his vegetarian diet, the Fuhrer watched much of the campaign's action firsthand from an aircraft window or an open automobile, including ground combat and Stuka bombardment in his itinerary. Films survive of Hitler watching from an aircraft, grim and expressionless, as explosions gut buildings in the Warsaw outskirts a few hundred feet below.

---

[64] Terry Brighton, 65.

Hitler in Poland with Rommel to his left

Technology and military doctrine both favored the Germans in the context of the era as well. The Germans considered communication key to good battlefield coordination and control, so radios were very commonplace. The Third Reich built large numbers of its tanks with individual radios, in contrast to the radio-free tanks of Poland. The Wehrmacht also made extensive use of radios in infantry units, and commanders, artillerymen, and spotters used radio communications to launch precise, timely fire missions to soften the way for their own attacks or halt those of the enemy.

Germany's army was far more mechanized than Poland's. Besides tanks and armored cars, a fleet of heavy trucks offered rapid transport of men and material. Halftracks moved artillery and ammunition to places where they were needed, and thousands of motorcycles with sidecars provided messenger service, scouting, and rapid deployment of machine gun teams. Statistics demonstrated the stark difference in mechanization between the opponents; 10% of the Polish army consisted of cavalry, while only 2% of the Wehrmacht was cavalry in 1939, a figure that was steadily shrinking too. Though a lack of fuel eventually proved the Achilles heel for German armies later in the war, this was not an issue during the Polish campaign of 1939.

As the days of the invasion wore on, Hitler used a Mercedes to travel to the front lines of the battle and to inspect the progress of the tanks as they moved across the Polish landscape to "retake" Danzig, a city the Germans believed had been stolen from them as a result of the Treaty of Versailles.[65] During this time, Rommel believed he was developing a relationship with Hitler, and he remarked in his letters to Lucie that he sometimes ate with the Fuhrer or was invited to lunch. As the weeks progressed, Rommel became aware that the special relationship was being noticed. He wrote, "I eat at his table twice each day now…Relations with [Colonel Rudolf] Schmundt are strained. Apparently my relationship with the Fuhrer is becoming too strong."[66] Strong enough, Rommel thought, to request that he be given the command of a Panzer (tank) division, though he had no experience in leading or serving in one.[67] Upon his eventual arrival at Bad Godesberg, one of his men wrote, "My infantry instructor from Dresden became our divisional commander. Much as we admired this man, we wondered if an infantryman could be a commander of tanks."[68]

The attack on Poland prompted Britain and France to enter the war, so the Nazi aggression therefore precipitated the spread of hostilities westward as well as eastward, extending the conflict around the globe as alliances triggered entry into the struggle like a series of diplomatic dominoes. Mussolini finally joined the Axis directly with the "Pact of Steel," the main effect of which was the creation of a third front in North Africa and Italy.

In 1939 and 1940, however, these developments mostly lay in the future, and Rommel had personally observed and learned much during the invasion of Poland. There, he developed several key ideas that would inform his leadership in Africa - it was better to strike hard, even if it involved risk, and move forward at every reasonable opportunity. The best use of tanks was to mass them at the front, and drive into the center of the fight, rather than spread them out in "penny packets" across the whole line.[69]

Chapter 5: Invading France with the Seventh Panzer Division

Much of World War I's most brutal action occurred in Belgium, including the region of Flanders, which also extends into northeastern France. The Allies sought to forestall the entire war by "blocking" Germany's westward advance through encouragement of Belgian neutrality, but this neutrality did nothing to stop the coming bloodbath. As fate would have it, history repeated itself a generation later when Belgium declared itself neutral, accidentally encouraging the Third Reich to invade its territories in the opening days of World War II. The moist, green Belgian countryside once again resounded to the shriek and crash of bombs, the thunder of artillery and tank guns, and the cries of wounded and dying men as the panzers and Stukas of Hitler's Third Reich plunged westward.

Initially, Hitler planned to begin heavy rearmament in earnest in 1943 to 1944, and he

---

[65] Ibid., 65-66.
[66] Ibid., 67.
[67] Ibid.
[68] Ibid., 72.
[69] Desmond Young, 67.

envisioned the Third Reich's confrontation with France and Britain happening somewhere from 1948-1950. However, the two nations' declaration of war following Hitler's brutal September annexation of Poland accelerated the timetable immensely. Hitler wanted to strike France in November 1939, but lack of sufficient materiel and planning difficulties delayed the invasion until May 1940.

After returning to Hitler's headquarters following the successful invasion of Poland, Rommel was given command of the 7th Panzer division on February 15th, 1940.[70] Rommel had just two months of training time before his division was to invade Belgium. Rommel quickly built a reputation for decisive action: "whatever mistakes he might make, [he] would make none from hesitating to 'have a go.'"[71] Rommel also showed himself willing to do what he asked of the men under his command. In the opening days of his command of the Seventh Panzers, he personally fell under heavy fire while assisting his men in the building of a bridge and in his personal tank, which was pinned down by anti-tank fire, an incident that could have resulted in his capture.[72]

The first decisive encounters of the German invasion of France in 1940 occurred not on French but on Belgian soil. As the strategy behind the Maginot Line made clear, French planning and strategy not only anticipated this but encouraged it in an effort to keep the Third Reich's military forces off French soil. Much of France's key industrial might operated on the northern coastal plain, so retaining this manufacturing capacity gave the French a better chance to win the conflict, remaining able to replace equipment losses rapidly. Seizure of the area would constitute a major prize for the Germans. Of course, the Belgians were far less enthusiastic about the scheme, which transformed their small country into a battlefield on which two larger nations would unleash the full fury of modern bombing, strafing, and tank warfare.

Tank warfare was still so new that the rules for Panzer divisions were being written in battle. Though orders were to withhold tank fire while the tank was in transit over concerns about wasted ammunition and inaccuracy, Rommel ordered his men to fire while rolling, believing that any truth to those concerns were "more than compensated by moral effect"[73] as the tanks moved across French lines and eventually into villages. The French, who were slower to activate their tanks, found them both rolled over and captured by the *blitzkrieg* war that had descended.[74]

The Germans arrived at the Meuse on May 12 largely free from harassment by Franco-British aircraft and were confronted by relatively weak defenses. Standing on the bank of the Meuse, Fedor von Bock confided to his diary, "Concerning Army Group A, the 4th Army has succeeded in crossing the Meuse near Yvoir and Dinant and has established bridgeheads there. The French

---

[70] Ibid., 71.
[71] Ibid., 72.
[72] Ibid., 71-72.
[73] Ibid., 73.
[74] Ibid.

really do seem to have taken leave of their senses." (Healy, 2008, 45). On May 13, Guderian's panzers crossed the Meuse almost unopposed, and the Germans launched a colossal Stuka dive-bomber attack of 500 sorties against the 55e Reserve Regiment, a low-quality French unit guarding the river near Sedan. General Maurice Gamelin, proving himself once again completely unfit to hold command, responded to requests for anti-aircraft guns to be sent to aid the 55e Regiment with the airy response that their squad machine guns would suffice to drive the Stukas away. These weapons, of course, lacked the range, accuracy, or striking power to even inconvenience the swiftly-descending Luftwaffe dive-bombers.

The stunned French found themselves under fire from the east bank by the deadly 88mm flak cannon, a German anti-aircraft gun which proved equally lethal against bunkers, buildings, and practically every type of armored vehicle fielded by the Allies during World War II. Guderian himself used a rubber assault boat to cross the Meuse after troops and engineers established a foothold on the west bank, and his subordinate, Lieutenant Colonel Balck, met him with a bit of jubilant, good-natured cheekiness as his boat approached shore. "He greeted me cheerfully with the cry 'Joy-riding in canoes on the Meuse is forbidden!' I had in fact used those words myself in one of the exercises that we had in preparation for this operation, since the attitude of some of younger officers had struck me as rather too light-hearted. I now realized that they had judged the situation correctly." (Evans, 2000, 52). Guderian's engineers threw three pontoon bridges across the Meuse at Wadelincourt, Glaire, and Donchery, and by midnight on the 13th, panzers poured across these temporary but expertly constructed bridges and moved on into the French countryside.

Meanwhile, Rommel's men arrived at the Meuse near Houx, a village close to Dinant, after fighting through unexpectedly stiff resistance on the eastern bank. Scouting carefully, the Germans found a long-abandoned weir connecting the two banks by way of a forested island in midstream. Waiting for complete darkness, a unit of German motorcycle troops drove their vehicles slowly across the river on the weir, establishing a bridgehead on the west bank. Though the French counterattacked strongly the next day with machine guns and mortar fire, the motorcycle soldiers maintained their foothold. Rommel's engineers rigged a cable ferry using pontoon boats intended for building a bridge, which allowed more infantry and armored vehicles to cross the Meuse, leading to expansion of the German foothold on the west bank and the eventual construction of complete pontoon bridges.

By the morning of May 14, Rommel's men moved away from the river. A handful of tanks and the 7th Rifle Regiment attacked the nearby town of Onhaye, which fell at 9:00 a.m. when 25 panzers from Panzer Regiment 25 completed the crossing at Houx and moved forward to encircle the town. The French defenders died or surrendered, giving Rommel control of a defensible position commanding the area around his crossing point. The 25th Panzer Regiment continued to spearhead the drive, reaching Morville by nightfall and extending the German position 6 miles into France.

May 14 witnessed French and British bombers and fighters attacking the pontoon bridges in the Ardennes, only to find themselves enveloped in a murderous cloud of flak. The Germans had not left their air defenses to squad machine-guns in the manner of Maurice Gamelin, instead deploying numerous flak batteries around all their river crossings. The aircraft sank two of Rommel's pontoons (though the engineers replaced them almost immediately) but inflicted no damage on Guderian's. Guderian himself reported on the futile courage of the Allied airmen: "There was now a most violent air attack by the enemy. The extremely brave French and English pilots did not succeed in knocking out the bridges, despite the heavy casualties that they suffered. Our anti-aircraft gunners proved themselves on this day, and shot superbly." (Evans, 2000, 60).

Suffering 50% or higher losses, the remaining aircraft limped back to their airfields, with many so shredded and battered by flak bursts that they proved no longer serviceable. The Germans now held an expanding slice of French territory, well away from the main Allied forces, and nothing the local defenders attempted sufficed to halt the Wehrmacht's swift, aggressive advance.

German soldiers crossing the Meuse on May 15

Rommel overlooking the 7th Panzer in France

Rommel made great territorial gains, and had relatively few losses to show during the French invasion. All told, the 7th Panzers had 35 killed, but took 10,000 prisoners, 130 tanks and armoured cars, and 27 guns, in a matter of two days.[75] Days later, in encountering the British for the first time, Rommel's losses would be heavier at 250 men. One of his fellow officers was

---

[75] Ibid., 75.

killed standing next to Rommel during the skirmish.[76]

After the Germans had forced the Meuse crossings OKW, the Wehrmacht high command, ordered Guderian to halt the Germans for 24 hours to give them time to rest, regroup, and refuel. However, Guderian decided to deliberately and thoroughly flout these orders; having gained a stunning advantage over the French, he declined to sacrifice it even to give his soldiers and himself much-needed rest. Guderian rightly figured that only by keeping up the pressure could the Panzer Divisions exploit the opportunities offered by running amok in the Allied rear.

Rommel found himself in the lead on May 15th, driving in his Kubelwagen staff car alongside much better protected panzers. The Germans pushed west and took a curving path northwest as they punched deep into French territory, aiming to reach the coast of the English Channel. In this way, the Wehrmacht would encircle the BEF and much of the French Army deployed in Belgium, putting them in an untenable position and hopefully forcing their surrender.

The Germans used forests – cleared of undergrowth for firewood like most European woodland at the time and therefore offering scant obstacle to tracked vehicles – to avoid air attacks, while bypassing towns where soldiers and anti-tank guns might delay their advance. Rommel pushed out far ahead of the main force but paused on a hill crest near sunset on May 15th to survey the landscape to his rear: "Looking back east from the summit of the hill, as night fell, endless pillars of dust could be seen rising as far as the eye could reach — comforting signs that the 7th Panzer Divisions move into the conquered territory had begun." (Evans, 2000, 70).

Rommel and Guderian continued their drive on the 16th, and the French forces showed strong signs of panic as the Germans pierced ever deeper into France. Many men encountered by the Wehrmacht made no effort to attack them, instead streaming down side roads in an attempt to escape. The Germans brushed past these and moved on as the French Army assumed the role of a traffic hazard rather than an active enemy force.

At this point, the OKW nearly scuppered the successful blitzkrieg from within. Field Marshal Paul von Kleist – eventually killed by the Russians for the crime of "alienating, through friendship and generosity, the peoples of the Soviet Union" – ordered Guderian to halt, fearing the overextended German advance would suffer counterattack and annihilation. Guderian tendered his resignation, thinking this would overcome Kleist's objections, but to his astonishment, Kleist accepted it. Ultimately, Gerd von Rundstedt adroitly averted this potential crisis of command by intervening with a solution; Rundstedt's plan called for Guderian to halt but permitted him to make a "reconnaissance in force." Rundstedt left the size and nature of this "reconnaissance" totally undefined, effectively writing Guderian a blank check to do whatever he wished so long as he made the conciliatory gesture of establishing a fixed headquarters and remaining there for a while.

---

[76] Ibid., 76.

On May 16th, the French command sent Colonel Charles de Gaulle to make a flanking attack with a tank force on the rapidly growing German salient. This, however, was too little, too late. De Gaulle found himself commanding a pitifully small force of tanks, but he nevertheless made a brave attempt to halt the Germans near Montcornet and Serre. After an initial success against light vehicles, the French found themselves under steady attack by artillery, Stuka dive-bombers, and mechanized infantry. Towards the end of the day, de Gaulle withdrew to spare his remaining men.

De Gaulle gathered more tanks and made a new attack at Crecy on May 19th, 1940, but he again suffered a violent repulse. The 19th witnessed another disaster for the French when the highly capable General Henri Giraud fell prisoner to the Germans, prompting his 9th Army to desert en masse within hours. General Maurice Gamelin, the commander who oversaw the disastrous French defense up to that point, held a feast for his leading officers and then relinquished overall command to General Maxime Weygand.

On May 20th, just 11 days after the commencement of hostilities, leading elements of the 2nd Panzer Division under Rudolf Veiel reached the coast at the commune of Noyelles-sur-Mer, close to the mouth of the Somme River. Guderian's bold advance had cut off three French armies and the British Expeditionary Force (BEF) successfully in Belgium and the northeast corner of France.

May 21 was something of a respite for both sides, due mainly to the indecisiveness of the leaders of both the Allied and Axis forces. Guderian's and Rommel's panzer divisions held their line, reinforcing it with motorized infantry and artillery, while the OKW attempted to decide whether to strike north against the encircled French and British forces or south into France proper. Eventually, the OKW decided on a northward advance, but the order arrived in mid-afternoon and Guderian could do little more than prepare his forces for the following day's advance.

One action on May 21st resulted from personal initiative on the part of BEF commander Field Marshal John Standish Surtees Prendergast Vereker, 6th Viscount Gort. From Arras, he launched an attack southward with two understrength British infantry divisions, 16 Matilda II tanks (capable of knocking out German armor), and several dozen weakly armed Matilda I tanks. Split into two columns, his small assault unit – dubbed the "Frankforce" – attacked Rommel's men near Wailly, Agny, and Beaurains. Lord Gort's diminutive Frankforce met with initial success, destroying a number of light Panzer I and II tanks, a convoy of trucks, some light A/T guns, and taking 400 German prisoners. The Matildas' thick armor stood them in good stead, deflecting lighter German shells and persuading many Wehrmacht soldiers, including Rommel himself, that they faced a far larger battalion of Allied juggernauts. As Rommel wrote, "The anti-tank guns which we quickly deployed showed themselves to be far too light to be effective against the heavily armoured British tanks, and the majority of them were put out of action by gunfire, together with their crews, and then overrun by the enemy tanks. Many of our vehicles were burnt out." (Horne, 383). Lord Gort's 60 to 70 tanks became "hundreds" in Rommel's mind, demonstrating that even the finest commanders can succumb to irrational fear. In fact, in Rommel's memoirs, he made the mistake of claiming that five full British armored divisions attacked him from Arras.

Nevertheless, the Germans concentrated several 88mm flak gun batteries in the path of the English and soon compelled the Frankforce to retreat, leaving 9 burning hulks behind, including two highly valuable Matilda IIs. On May 22, Rommel attacked north towards Arras. A spoiling attack pinned him down for a while, but on the 23rd, he took the city and advanced past it. Guderian also sent a pair of panzer divisions north, aiming to seize Calais and Boulogne. Lord Gort and Maxime Weygand failed to meet and devise a plan, an event ascribed to the British commander's malice by the French but which actually resulted from appallingly bad communications.

Prime Minister Paul Reynaud announced the desperate situation to the French Senate in Paris that day, producing deep shock. Most government officials of France believed, up to that moment, in an imminent Allied victory. The Secretary of War, Marshal Petain – later head of the collaborationist Vichy government – argued for an armistice. Nevertheless, Weygand remained confident, albeit for reasons that might have been comical if not for the situation's deadly seriousness: "Despite his arduous experiences of the past twenty-four hours, the seventy-three-year-old Generalissimo arrived full of bounce and launched into his analysis of the situation on an evident note of optimism. 'So many mistakes have been made,' he began, 'that they give me confidence. I believe that in future we shall make less.'" (Horne, 2007, 389).

Weygand outlined a plan of bizarre optimism in which the entire trapped Allied force would turn south and "round up" the panzers in the course of one day. In the meantime, the Germans established numerous bridgeheads on the south bank of the Somme, to be used when the southward advance began. Panzers invested Boulogne on May 22nd, and on May 23rd, the British evacuated their troops at midnight. The French garrison surrendered at noon two days later on May 25th, recognizing their utterly hopeless position.

The British government ordered an evacuation of Dunkirk on May 26th, but the British Expeditionary Force (BEF) and the French forces accompanying them could not escape that easily, however. Near catastrophe struck on May 28th when the Belgians surrendered to Germany, opening a colossal gap in the Allied lines. King Leopold III, showing consistency of character at least if not moral courage, informed the British and French of his planned capitulation only hours prior to the actual surrender, leaving them with practically no time to prepare for its disastrous military consequences. The action earned Leopold III such sobriquets as "King Rat" and "the Traitor King," nicknames he did little to disprove when he evinced more willingness to negotiate with Hitler for restoration of Belgian independence than he had shown in dealing with France and Britain, which sought to defend Belgium's freedom in the first place. British Prime Minister Sir Winston Churchill blasted the Belgian monarch's abrupt surrender in a detailed speech summarizing the repercussions: "The surrender of the Belgian Army compelled the British at the shortest notice to cover a flank to the sea more than 30 miles in length. Otherwise all would have been cut off, and all would have shared the fate to which King Leopold had condemned the finest army his country had ever formed. So in doing this and in exposing this flank, as anyone who followed the operations on the map will see, contact was lost between the British and two out of the three corps forming the First French Army." (Churchill, 2013, 174).

The BEF and their French allies in Dunkirk owed their escape to an unlikely source: the bombastic Luftwaffe leader, Hermann Goering. Goering wanted the glory of destroying the trapped Allies for the Luftwaffe and persuaded Hitler to order the panzer divisions to halt. Without this error, the "Miracle of Dunkirk" – also known as "Operation Dynamo" – would likely have failed, and the Germans may have taken vast numbers of English and French prisoners, possibly ending British participation in the war.

Meanwhile, Rommel pressed on to Cherbourg, and though he faced some resistance along the way, the fortress there, as well as 30,000 Frenchmen, surrendered to his Panzer division on June 19th. By the time the French had surrendered, Rommel and his 7th Panzers had compiled an impressive list of damage they had inflicted on the enemy: "They took 97,468 prisoners, shot down 52 aircraft, destroyed 15 more on the ground, and captured a dozen airplanes intact. They captured Admiral Abrial, the commander of the French Atlantic fleet, and four other admirals, a French corps commander, the commander of the British 51st Infantry Division, about twenty other generals, and a number of headquarters and supply staffs. They also bagged 277 field guns, 64 antitank guns, 458 tanks and armored cars, 4,000 to 5,000 trucks, 1,500 to 2,000 cars, a similar number of horse and mule wagons, 300 to 400 buses, and about the same number of military motorcycles."[77]

---

[77] Samuel W. Mitcham, Jr., *Rommel's Greatest Victory: The Desert Fox and the Fall of Tobruk, Spring 1942* (Novato, CA: Presidio Press, 1998), 15.

Chapter 6: 1941

Rommel in North Africa in 1941

"The Italian command was, for the most part, not equal to the task of carrying on war in the desert, where the requirement was lightning decision followed by immediate action. The training of the Italian infantryman fell far short of the standard required by modern warfare. … Particularly harmful was the all pervading differentiation between officer and man. While the men had to make shift without field-kitchens, the officers, or many of them, refused adamantly to forgo their several course meals. Many officers, again, considered it unnecessary to put in an appearance during battle and thus set the men an example. All in all, therefore, it was small wonder that the Italian soldier, who incidentally was extraordinarily modest in his needs,

developed a feeling of inferiority which accounted for his occasional failure and moments of crisis. There was no foreseeable hope of a change for the better in any of these matters, although many of the bigger men among the Italian officers were making sincere efforts in that direction."
- Rommel

Rommel was sent to Africa in February 1941 after the Italian armies there had been easily defeated by the British. The British armies, though small in number at about 30,000, had systematically destroyed the Italian Tenth Army in Egypt and Libya. Though Mussolini had hoped for miraculous victories that would impress Hitler and allow the Italians to join the Germans in the division of Hitler's *blitzkrieg*-acquired lands, the Italian army was one of the most poorly prepared in Europe. Instead, a huge number of Italian soldiers suffered casualties, were taken as prisoners of war after losing battles, or simply surrendered to the British without a fight.[78] As a result of the stunning losses that destroyed Italy's forces in less than two months,[79] Rommel correctly surmised, "The Italian troops had, with good reason, lost all confidence in their arms and acquired a very serious inferiority complex, which was to remain with them throughout the whole war."[80]

In January 1941, the Italian armies, seeking refuge in their retreat, had taken their place in two fortresses at Bardia and Tobruk. Here, the Italians hoped the humiliation they had suffered in battle could be stopped, as the African strongholds were considered to be very defensible and were commanded by Italy's most formidable generals. Instead, they were soundly defeated, and with that the British were the undisputed masters of Egypt and had a secure hold in North Africa. Desmond Young, Rommel's most famous biographer, writes of the stunning defeat of the British armies only two months later: "If, in the early summer of 1941, one had stopped the first passer-by in the streets of Cairo and asked him the reason for this astonishing reversal of fortune, it is odds-on that he would have replied in one word: Rommel."[81]

Upon his arrival in Africa, Rommel set into motion plans to retake the areas lost to the British, Cyrenaica specifically, by April. The British believed that Rommel would be completely unable to mount an offense before May, but he would soon surprise both the British and his own countrymen. As "a man who considered the enemy's sound estimate of the possible as the main ingredient of his own success,"[82] Rommel would become known for wasting no time.

Desert fighting conditions were something that every general and soldier arriving in North Africa had to get used to (a fact that the British generals believed the British War Cabinet ignored), and Rommel was no exception. He described his first sandstorm thusly: "Immense red clouds of reddish dust obscured all visibility and forced the car's speed down to a crawl. Sand

---

[78] Ibid.,1-8.
[79] Ibid., 8.
[80] Ibid.
[81] Desmond Young, 22.
[82] Correlli Barnett, *The Desert Generals* (New York: Viking Press, 1961), 63.

streamed down the windscreen like water. We gasped in our breath through handkerchiefs held over our faces and sweat poured off our bodies in the unbearable heat."[83]

It was here, in the desert, that Rommel began to wear what would become his trademark goggles, always across his general's cap. While some biographers claim Rommel had retrieved the goggles from an abandoned British vehicle, stating that "even a general was allowed a little booty," a 2015 *Daily Mail* article claims that a British POW actually gave his goggles to the general. After his capture, Major General Michael Gambier-Parry was invited to supper with Rommel, where he informed the field marshal that his hat had been stolen by a German soldier. Rommel investigated, and returned Gambier-Parry's hat, but asked if he could keep the British-issue goggles that the general had left in his staff car.[84] They became part of his signature appearance, and he was rarely photographed without them after 1941. Rommel would also receive his moniker, the Desert Fox, in the weeks following his victories there. In German *"Wustenfuchs,"* it described a "small fox with a habit of burrowing quickly into the sand to escape predators, affording human occupants of the desert only an occasional fleeting glance."[85]

On March 31, 1941, Rommel struck, despite his orders to wait for the arrival of two additional Panzer divisions. Ironically, the British advantage in having cracked the German Enigma Code actually hurt them because they initially acted on the assumption that Rommel would follow orders to stop his advance. In his initial forays into battle, he had almost unbelievable success, capturing a key British general, destroying a British division, and capturing the city of Benghazi in modern day Libya.[86] He began pushing the British forces back over 1,000 miles, snatching victory in the Middle East from British hands.[87] In a letter to Lucie, Rommel described his decision and its results, predicting, "The top brass in Rome and Berlin will be shocked. I have dared to go on, against orders, because I saw what might be won. The British are on the run. I cannot sleep for joy."[88]

The next victory for Rommel would be harder won. Intent on taking the fortress of Tobruk, Rommel struck immediately with the belief that the frightened British were preparing to evacuate their troops by sea. Instead, the ships were supplying the Brits, and Winston Churchill had ordered Tobruk to be "held to the death with no thought of retirement."[89] Initial attempts to storm the fortress were unsuccessful, and even resulted in General Johannes Streich refusing another attack in the face of heavy losses. This angered Rommel, and he reported to Berlin, "My clear and specific orders were not obeyed by my commanders, and some commanders broke down in the face of the enemy."[90]

---

[83] Terry Brighton, 98.
[84] Hannah Flint, "Revealed: Desert Fox Erwin Rommel was given his legendary goggles by a British POW in return for retrieving a stolen hat." *The UK Daily Mail Online.* April 20, 2015. Accessed August 6, 2016.
[85] Terry Brighton, 100.
[86] Samuel Mitcham Jr., *Rommel's Greatest Victory.*, 16.
[87] Ibid., 18.
[88] Terry Brighton, 99.
[89] Ibid., 101.

Streich

The British attempted to "finish off" Rommel for the first time with Operation Battleaxe in June of 1941. Despite their advantages in this battle, Rommel used defensive, rather than offensive, measures to destroy British tanks, taking out 11 of the 12 British tanks in the initial minutes of the operation. Rommel refused to fight the British on their terms, relying, instead, on his anti-aircraft guns to destroy British tanks on the field of battle and in reserve. He would once ask a captured Brit, "What does it matter if you have two tanks to my one, when you spread them

---

[90] Ibid.

out and let me smash them unit by unit?"[91] The British were forced to inform Churchill of "the failure of Battleaxe."[92] Meanwhile, Rommel received Hitler's praise and a promotion to General of Panzer troops. He informed Lucie, "I owe my rapid promotion to the Fuhrer…You can understand how very pleased I am."[93]

After these actions, Rommel gave up on assaults and instead laid siege to Tobruk. During the 242 day standoff, the British were intent on disrupting the supply lines in order to starve out Rommel's men. They were very successful in this, sinking over 77% of the supplies that Rommel badly needed, in November of 1941.[94] On the 18th of November, with Rommel having just arrived from a two-day break and celebration of his 50th birthday with Lucie in Rome,[95] the British began what the Germans called the "winter battle," with Rommel's poorly-supplied men facing "the most complex and fluid [battle] of World War II" with under 300 tanks, in comparison to the British forces' 1,000.

Again, though Rommel faced incredible odds, he was able to stave off the British advance until December. With that said, while Rommel's victories were impressive, they cost him in terms of both men and equipment. The lack of viable supply lines meant that he would eventually have to give up the siege of Tobruk, in the face of an "Afrika Korps…down to a strength of 80 operational tanks…[and having] lost all three of his German divisional commanders…38,300 men were killed, wounded, and captured--32 percent of his original force."[96] The siege of Tobruk was abandoned on December 5th, 1941.[97]

Chapter 7: Reinforcements

"Courage which goes against military expediency is stupidity, or, if it is insisted upon by a commander, irresponsibility." - Rommel

Cognizant of Rommel's supply situation, the British believed they had been victorious in North Africa and began to spread out their forces to "finish the job,"[98] but the Italians were able to supply Rommel, and in January of 1942, he planned a surprise attack on the British lines, writing to his wife, "I've decided to take the risk [and strike again]. I have complete faith that God is keeping a protective hand over us and that He will grant us victory."[99] Just four weeks after the British had held onto Tobruk and the Germans were in retreat, the fortunes of the armies had been reversed. Rommel retook Benghazi, and congratulated his men: "Soldiers of the Panzerarmee Afrika! A great battle has been won. The enemy has lost his powerful armor. Now

---

[91] Ibid., 109.
[92] Ibid., 103.
[93] Ibid.
[94] Samuel Mitcham Jr., *Rommel's Greatest Victory*, 18-19.
[95] Terry Brighton, 107.
[96] Samuel Mitcham Jr., *Rommel's Greatest Victory*, 20.
[97] Terry Brighton, 109
[98] Samuel Mitcham Jr., *Rommel's Greatest Victory*, 21.
[99] Ibid.

we will shatter the last remnants of the British Eighth Army."[100]

It was from the Cyrencenian airfields that the British supplied Malta. If the Malta forces could not be used to block supply lines to the Germans, the British had little hope of stemming the tide of victories for an increasingly strong German force. Taking Benghazi back was therefore necessary.[101]

When Rommel arrived in Africa, it was vital that he make an impression on the Allied soldiers. The impression was great, so much so that Rommel's reputation as a general became legend, not just among his own men, but amongst the British, as well. British General Claude Auchinleck, having replaced General Wavell (whom Churchill perceived to be failing), recognized the development and its danger to British morale when he issued the following to "all commanders and chiefs of staff": "There exists a real danger that our friend Rommel is becoming a kind of magical or bogey-man to our troops, who are talking far too much about him. He is by no means a superman, although he is undoubtedly very energetic and able. Even if he were a superman, it would still be highly undesirable that our men should credit him with supernatural powers. I wish you to dispel by all possible means the idea that Rommel represents something more than an ordinary German general. The important thing now is to see to it that we do not always talk of Rommel when we mean the enemy in Libya. We must refer to "the Germans" or "the axis powers" or "the enemy" and not always keep harping on Rommel. Please ensure that this order is put into immediate effect, and impress upon all Commanders that, from a psychological point of view, it is a matter of the highest importance."[102]

---

[100] Terry Brighton, 113.
[101] Samuel Mitcham Jr., *Rommel's Greatest Victory*, 25.
[102] Ibid., 23.

Auchinleck

Samuel W. Mitcham Jr. writes of the striking contrast between the leaders of Germany and Britain when it came to the North African theatre. Winston Churchill was in conflict with Auchinleck over what Churchill believed to be his overly cautious approach, and demanded that Auchinleck go on the offensive as soon as possible to defend and supply Malta. Auchinleck refused, stating that his armies were unprepared for desert fighting. The conflict grew so intense that Churchill flatly demanded Auchinleck move or resign.

Rommel, in contrast, was allowed more autonomy, but with it came a general ignorance about the importance of Africa to the war in general. Rommel returned to Germany and an audience with Hitler, in July of 1941, during which he asked for reinforcements—a request that was refused--and made his case for taking Tobruk, followed by Cairo and the Suez Canal.[103] Instead of being taken seriously, Rommel was made to feel that his visit had been unnecessary, likely because the German Wehrmacht had attacked the Soviet Union in June in Operation Barbarossa, and now had bigger problems of concern.[104]

---

[103] Terry Brighton, 104.
[104] Samuel Mitcham Jr.., 27-28.

Rommel and staff in Africa in 1942

Chapter 8: El Alamein

In June of 1942, the British retreated to El Alamein, there to organize a "last stand."[105] Churchill was on the defensive with both the House of Commons and his countrymen after the loss of Tobruk and a bleak outlook for North Africa. For those losses, he gave credit to Rommel, claiming, "We have a very daring and skillful opponent against us, and may I say across the havoc of war, a great general."[106] Though the Germans were losing on the eastern front and concentrating their military efforts there, the German propaganda machine led by Joseph Goebbels made sure that Rommel was the one making headlines. It was unfortunate for Rommel that the commitment to North Africa was only skin deep.

Rommel was growing increasingly frustrated with the lack of the Reich's understanding of the situation in North Africa. In a meeting with Hitler in 1942, he advised that the theatre be abandoned. Hitler refused, but sensing Rommel's desperation, reassured him that the Reich would do everything possible to win the fight. Rommel and Goering were sent to Rome by train to inspect the situation.[107] It was on this trip that Rommel began to grow even more despondent, calling Goering his "bitterest enemy."[108] Both Rommel and Lucie were "horrified" by Goering's

---

[105] Terry Brighton, 113.
[106] Ibid., 114.
[107] Heinrich Fraenkel and Roger Manvell. *Goering: The Rise and Fall of the Notorious Nazi Leader*. (London: Frontline Books, 2011). 270.

behavior throughout the trip, where he lectured anyone willing to listen on his understanding of art and sculpture, the collections he was amassing, and his fine taste for emerald jewelry. Lucie believed his behavior was akin to megalomania, though he promised her that the party leadership "[were] going to look after [Rommel]. We are going to do everything for him."[109] The topic of Africa, though, was avoided at all costs.[110]

Historian Terry Brighton explains both Rommel's success and his limits as a commander: "Where equal forces met, Rommel's genius gave him the advantage. The tide would turn if enemy forces outnumbered him by a considerable degree. With the loss of his natural tactical advantage any war of attrition could go against him. That was about to happen at El Alamein."[111]

Montgomery believed that while his troops had been engaged in fighting with the Germans for a lengthy period of time, they lacked proper training and a proper understanding of military maneuvers, so in the fall of 1942, units which were recalled from the front lines for "rest" were subjected to training regimens that were supposed to prepare them for the large-scale engagements that he had planned for the future. As one soldier noted when he was recalled from the front lines to a rest area, "In a rest area you either dug holes all day and guarded dumps all night or you trained all day and guarded dumps all night. This rest area was different. You trained all day and then you trained all night. Not every day and every night – but almost." (Latimer, p. 120) However, when Churchill learned that Montgomery was delaying offensive operations to train his troops, he became furious. Churchill believed the British needed to press the Germans, in part because he wanted the British to beat the Germans before relying on American assistance, and he had fired Auchinleck in part because he often needed to be goaded into attacking.

As it turned out, Montgomery's delays were fortuitous, because the Germans suffered a huge blow in late September 1942 when Rommel was forced to return to Germany after suffering from various ailments that finally caught up to him. He described his situation to Lucie: "much too low blood pressure, state of exhaustion, six to eight weeks' rest recommended," but high-command refused, leaving him no choice but to attack.[112] Rommel did so with huge misgivings, confiding in his doctor that his "decision to attack today is the hardest I have ever taken. Either the army in Russia succeeds in getting through to Grozny and we in Africa manage to reach the Suez Canal, or…at that…[Rommel made a gesture of defeat]."[113]

---

[108] Ibid.
[109] Desmond Young, 196.
[110] Ibid., 271.
[111] Terry Brighton, 115.
[112] Ibid., 124.
[113] Ibid., 125.

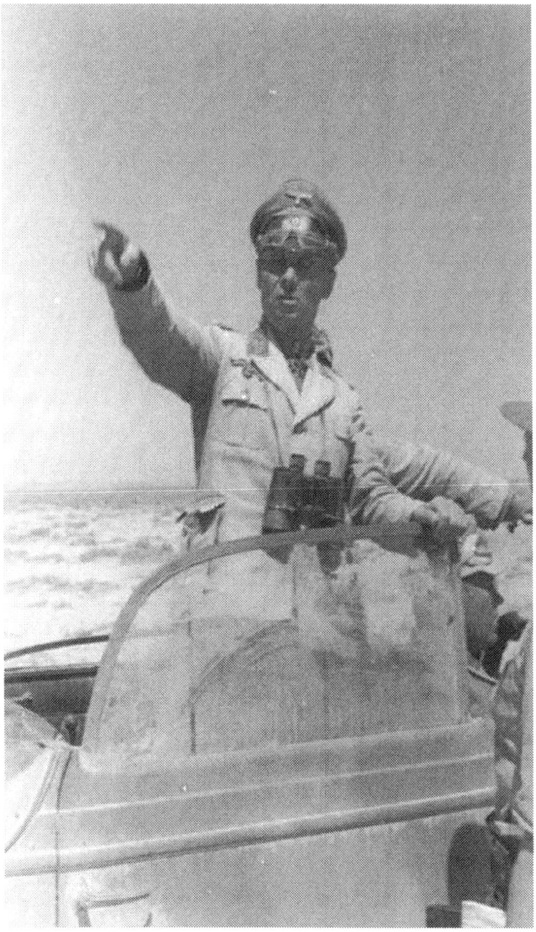

Bundesarchiv, Bild 146-1977-018-11A
Foto: Zwilling, Ernst A. | Juni 1942

Pictures of Rommel in 1942

Although Rommel had been dealing with circulation and blood-pressure problems, chronic stomach and intestinal catarrh, and nasal diphtheria, he most likely would not have left his command but for the fact he was convinced a British attack would not occur for 6-8 weeks, which would give him a window to return to Germany, recover, and then return to North Africa. When he reached Berlin to begin his recuperation, Rommel found that his reputation and previous victories actually hurt him, because his requests for more supplies and manpower in North Africa were rejected by military officials who pointed to his ability to do more with less.

Georg Stumme replaced Rommel in the interim, but before he left, Rommel created a defensive plan for his forces that abandoned the mobile tactics they had been so successful with in previous engagements. With the Royal Air Force dominating the skies and the extremely low supplies of fuel that the Germans had on hand, Rommel instead decided to create a web of static defensive positions encircled by minefields that would allow the Germans to withstand Anglo-American attacks and then quickly launch counterattacks. The outer edges of the German defense were wired and mined to a depth of between 500 and 1,000 yards. After that, the Germans positioned weapon pits for machine-gun and light mortars, then a second minefield, and finally, the main German defensive positions. The Germans laid a total of 249,849 anti-tank mines and 14,509 anti-personnel mines.

Stumme

In terms of total troop strength, the Axis army in North Africa now consisted of four German divisions and eight Italian divisions, along with the German-Italian Panzer Army that consisted of the 15th and 21st Panzer Divisions, the 90th Light Division, the 164th Division, the Ramcke Parachute Brigade, and three Italian corps (the X, XX, and XXI. Rommel had serious doubts about the effectiveness of his Italian forces, so whenever he was given the opportunity, he sandwiched Italian units between German units in order to "stiffen the Italians' resolve."

While the Germans dug in on defense, the British also prepared for a major engagement by secretly moving men and weaponry forward from the rear. From September 6 - October 22, flights of 20-30 bombers flew missions over German and Italian cities like Tobruk, Matruh,

Sollum, Bardia, Benghazi, and even as far away as Suda Bay (Crete) and Navarino (southwest Greece). On October 9, a heavy raid on Luftwaffe airfields all but ended their effectiveness in North Africa, and heavy bombing by Royal Air Force planes signaled the beginning of Britain's offensive. Planes spent the next five days continuously bombing German and Italian positions, while on the ground, British, New Zealand, and Australian units moved into position. On the morning of October 23rd, the 21st Squadron Royal Engineers were briefed as to their role: "I know I'm speaking to young men only 20 or 21 years old, but I have to give it to you straight: right behind you is a whole division relying on you sappers to open the lanes for the tanks and infantry to pass through. Also behind you are a thousand guns. They will put up a terrific barrage as you sappers go in. Some of you will be killed, or lose an arm or leg, because Jerry will be trying to stop you. There will be mortaring, Stuka dive bombing and the rest." (Latimer, p. 174)

As they began heavy artillery fire and aerial bombardment to soften the Axis defenses, British troops made final preparations for the battle ahead, but as one soldier noted, the "prelude to the battle was a nightmare…we worked from dusk to dawn each night, and as the flies and heat made it virtually impossible to sleep during the day, we entered the battle in a fair state of exhaustion. Working conditions were appalling: the Alamein position had been fought over several times and the whole area was littered with decomposing corpses, some unburied and others whose graves had been uncovered by the wind. The stench of putrefaction was all-pervading and the air thick with dust and horrible desert flies." (Latimer, p. 171)

On the eve of battle, British forces enjoyed overwhelming tank superiority over the Germans and Italians. The British had 1,029 tanks at the front (267 of which were Shermans, advanced enough to be able to stand their ground against the German Panzer Mark IV "Specials"), as well as another 200 tanks in reserve. The Germans only had 218 operational tanks, while the Italians had 278. The British superiority was therefore more than 2:1, which was an important advantage but still less than the 3:1 ratio that was generally believed necessary to attack prepared positions. Naturally, British troops were on edge all day on October 23, and as one soldier recalled: "Perhaps the worst of the suspense was over…"

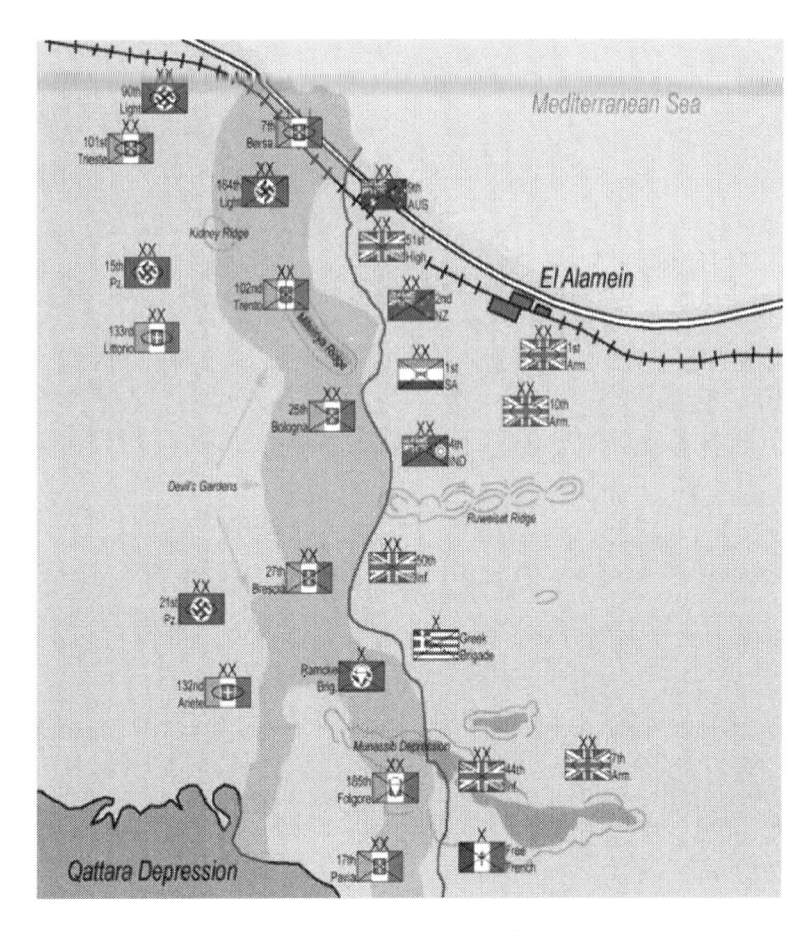

The lines at the start of the Second Battle of El Alamein

The next morning, when the pre-attack artillery barrage began, 882 field and medium guns participated in softening up the Axis' forward positions. An Allied soldier recalled, "No fury of sound had ever assailed our ears like that before, it cuffed, shattered and distorted the senses, and loosened the bowels alarmingly. I was more than startled, I was shocked, and needed to know that everyone else was there. When I could focus, the faces I saw first looked blanched and then flushed brightly in a kaleidoscope of passionately flickering hues as every line and every detail was etched into relief by the flashes from muzzles of the guns…hundreds of guns almost hub to hub, all bucking, recoiling, spitting fire and snapping like a pack of vicious terriers, all at once, it was sheer horror…The constant drill by which our army life had been ruled was now our saving grace, and even before the initial shock had been fully absorbed we fell into the routine of performing all our tasks automatically." (Latimer, p. 177)

A picture of the Allied artillery barrage to start the battle

After the Allies fired over half a million shells, the attack, dubbed Operation Lightfoot, began with infantry advancing and engineers clearing the mines for the tanks. By 0200 on the 24th, 500 tanks began advancing forward, but across various parts of the line, the Allies were surprised by the depth of the German minefields, which slowed the attack. Nonetheless, Montgomery still hoped to break through in the north and begin a rout.

A German mine explodes as Allied tanks cross a minefield.

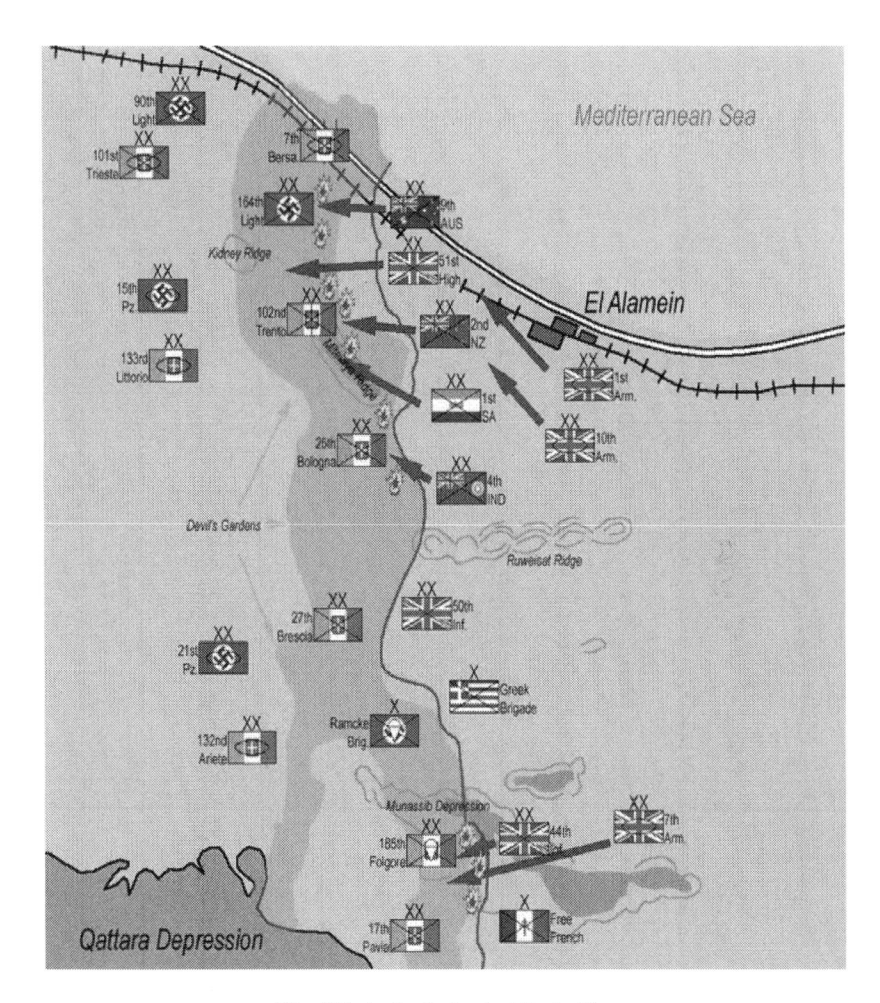

The Allied attacks to start the battle.

Although Rommel was rushing back to the front from Germany almost as soon as the battle started, the Germans suffered a disaster when Stumme apparently suffered a heart attack after coming under enemy fire during the 24th. With Stumme dead and Rommel at least a few days away from arriving, the Germans were deprived of their two most important commanders as the Allies cleared mines and gradually pushed forward throughout the 24th. All the while, the Royal Air Force ran sorties that softened up Axis positions.

Allied bombing at El Alamein.

On October 25th, as the British were shifting operations to the northwest, an Axis counterattack against the London Rifle Brigade created a short but crucial engagement in which Axis tanks, including Italian M13s and German Mark IIIs, engaged the Rifle Brigade's infantry units' dug-in positions that were supported by anti-tank guns. The Axis tanks were trying to utilize their superior firepower against what they believed was a weak spot in the British line manned only by infantry, but anti-tank fire halted their forward momentum, and as their tanks were hit, the crews tried to escape: "One Italian officer was hoisting himself out when a 6-pounder shot hit him in the chest and he literally disintegrated." In their withdrawal from the engagement, Axis units were forced to leave 14 tanks behind. This counterattack revealed the Axis strategy of trying to engage infantry units with tanks, but it also showed the problems tank attacks had when fighting dug-in infantry positions effectively supported by anti-tank guns. Even if successful, their tank strength would be depleted, and with an already unfavorable tank ratio against the British, this strategy might gain the Germans and Italians some territory, but they would still lose in terms of material strength.

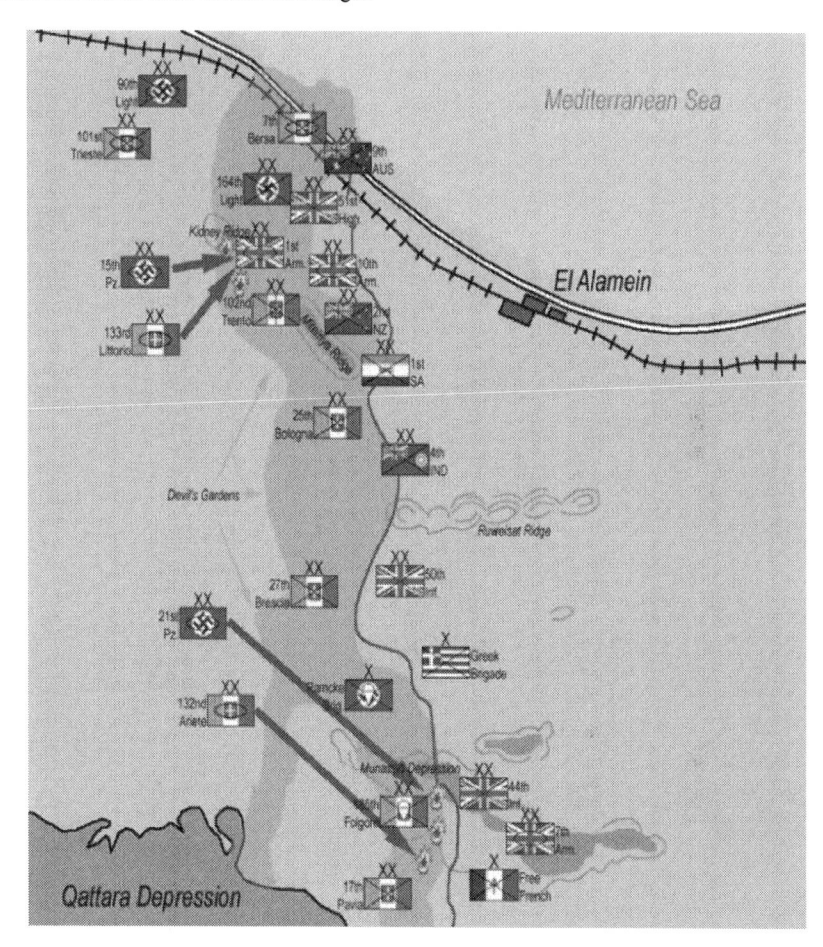

The Axis counterattack

Late on the 25th, Rommel returned to take command of the Axis forces, but he found the situation to be critical. British artillery had done heavy damage to the German and Italian defensive lines, and while they had prevented a breakthrough, they were unable to dislodge the enemy from their positions. Additionally, Axis forces were suffering from fuel shortages that were limiting what they were able to accomplish. As one officer told Rommel, "The fuel situation permitted only local counter-attacks by our panzer units which were standing ready immediately behind the threatened sectors of the front." He also explained, "Only small supplies of fuel remain close to the front." (Latimer, p. 230)

As the battle raged on, infantrymen and anti-tank crews attempted to stem the Axis counterattack and hold their position. One Allied soldier described the scene: "[O]ne of our [anti-tank] chaps crawls from his trench and with bullets ripping into the sand around him, runs stooping over to a 6-pounder fronting north, extracts a shell already in the breech and creeps back with it to his own gun which faces the panzer. It's amazing how the [machine-gun] stream misses him, but he calmly puts the shell in, takes steady aim, and fires. Immediately there's an explosion from the panzer." (Latimer, p. 252) As the engagement ended, Axis forces had lost 70 tanks, while the British forces lost 16 carriers and 10 guns, along with a large number of infantry deaths.

A disabled British Sherman tank at the battle.

The Axis command, realizing the dire situation they were in, ordered a number of counterattacks that were halted by British artillery fire, but both Montgomery and Churchill were frustrated by the inability to push forward faster, and at one point Churchill complained, "Is it really impossible to find a general who can win a battle?" After a few days of action that did not provide a decisive breakthrough, Montgomery ordered a new attack, codenamed Supercharge, that would take place on November 1. Meanwhile, Montgomery sought to consolidate the gains that his troops had made in the north by resuming operations in the south. To do this, he brought his New Zealand divisions back into action, where they would be supported by the 2nd

Armoured Brigade, the 7th Motor Brigade, and the 8th Armoured Brigade. As they moved out, one soldier recalled, "As far as could be seen, to both left and right of us, men were advancing with their rifles in the porte position, their bayonets glinting in the pale moonlight. Full moon had been days ago so it was quite dark…As we advanced, the feeling of pride and exhilaration was unmistakable. We didn't realize or think of the danger we were in; we were doing a job and the thought of being killed or wounded was far from our minds…I remember seeing forms sink to the ground but our orders were to keep going and not to stop for wounded or dying. Later we passed slit trenches with forms slouched over them facing in our direction … " (Latimer, p. 284)

Although the Australians were unable to break through at the beginning of the operation, over the next few days, the Allies managed to drive a wedge into the Axis positions, and with Rommel's panzer strength dwindling, there were basically no reinforcements at his disposal to plug the hole in his lines. Montgomery later reported, "If the British armour owed any debt to the infantry of the Eighth Army, the debt was paid on November 2 by 9th Armoured in heroism and blood." In the drive forward, the 9th Armoured lost 70 vehicles and more than half of their tank crew of 400 men. When one Allied general asked the 9th Armoured's leader, John Cecil Currie, where his tanks were, Currie pointed to a small group of tanks. When the general responded, "I don't mean your headquarters tanks, I mean your armoured regiments. Where are they?" Currie explained, "There are my armoured regiments…"

By the evening of November 2, Rommel began ordering a withdrawal of his forces, and he sent an aide to deliver a message to Hitler that read, "The army's strength was so exhausted after its ten days of battle that it was not now capable of offering any effective opposition to the enemy's next break-through attempt...With our great shortage of vehicles an orderly withdrawal of the non-motorised forces appeared impossible...In these circumstances we had to reckon, at the least, with the gradual destruction of the army." Despite telling Hitler that the battle was inevitably lost, Rommel received a directive on the afternoon of November 3: "To Field Marshal Rommel. It is with trusting confidence in your leadership and the courage of the German-Italian troops under your command that the German people and I are following the heroic struggle in Egypt. In the situation which you find yourself there can be no other thought but to stand fast, yield not a yard of ground and throw every gun and every man into the battle. Considerable air force reinforcements are being sent to C.-in-C South. The Duce and the Comando Supremo are also making the utmost efforts to send you the means to continue the fight. Your enemy, despite his superiority, must also be at the end of his strength. It would not be the first time in history that a strong will has triumphed over the bigger battalions. As to your troops, you can show them no other road than that to victory or death. Adolf Hitler"

This forced Rommel to stop his order to withdraw and uphold Hitler's order that "you can show no other road than that of victory or death." Late that night, as Rommel grappled with Hitler's orders, he discussed the situation with Major Elmar Warning and reached the conclusion that following Hitler would be suicidal: "If I do obey the Führrer's order then there's the danger that my troops won't obey me…The Führer is crazy." (Latimer, p. 296)

Due to Rommel's initial orders and Hitler's response urging the Desert Fox to remand them, Axis forces along the front were in a state of flux. Rommel initially attempted to halt the order to withdraw after it had been in effect for 15 hours and ordered his troops to stand firm, but then he began to waffle over whether to disobey Hitler's directive. Ultimately, he ordered a partial withdrawal to a prepared position behind their lines. Naturally, this left Rommel's troops in a state of confusion and chaos; some troops had already been withdrawn, and then the back and forth movement of transports and carriers that his orders had caused created congestion that made it impossible for effective troop movement. As this was going on, the thin line of German and Italian troops on the front line continued trying to hold off the British advance.

By the early hours of November 4th, a number of British regiments had made decisive breakthroughs against the Italian divisions in the north, and by daybreak on the 4th, British commanders received news of victory. Rommel reported, "The picture in the early afternoon of the 4th was as follows: powerful enemy armoured forces…had burst a 19-kilometre hole in our front, through which strong bodies of tanks were moving to the west. As a result of this, our forces in the north were threatened with encirclement by enemy formations 20 times their number in tanks ... There were no reserves, as every available man and gun had been put into the line. So now it had come, the thing we had done everything in our power to avoid – our front broken and the fully motorised enemy streaming into our rear. Superior orders could no longer count. We had to save what there was to be saved."

As Allied units chased the Italians across the desert, they had to surrender en masse due to their lack of ammunition and other resources like food and water. A writer for *Time* magazine wrote that for the Italians, It was a terrific letdown by their German allies. They had fought a good fight. In the south, the famed Folgore parachute division fought to the last round of ammunition. Two armoured divisions and a motorised division, which had been interspersed among the German formations, thought they would be allowed to retire gracefully with Rommel's 21st, 15th and 19th light. But even that was denied them. When it became obvious to Rommel that there would be little chance to hold anything between El Daba and the frontier, his Panzers dissolved, disintegrated and turned tail, leaving the Italians to fight a rear-guard action."

After the decisive victory at Alamein, British forces in North Africa engaged in mopping up duties against Axis forces that they pursued across the region to El Agheila. By the time the battle technically ended on November 11, the Allies had knocked out over 500 tanks and inflicted over 30,000 casualties, while losing less than 15,000 men and somewhere between 350-500 tanks. Given that the Axis had the advantage of defense, the fact that both sides lost an equal amount of tanks was an impressive feat for the Allies, especially given their overwhelming material advantage.

The victory at El Alamein was incredibly decisive for a number of reasons. First, it showed the

Allies the importance of a strategy that involved artillery and air-support, and that the Allies were superior to the Axis forces in this regard. Later in the war, as they fought in the European theater, German prisoners of war asked to see the "artillery machine gun" that the Allies had in their arsenal and were shocked to find that the rapid firing artillery that they so feared was not due to new technology but simply the skill of Allied artillery units. The campaign in North Africa also revealed the importance of "administration"; While Rommel revealed himself to be a master tactician, Alamein, like Stalingrad and the Marne, showed the importance of staying within the army's supply lines and not over-extending.

Last but certainly not least, the success at Alamein was vital to the British psyche, as it was their first permanent victory. Fittingly, Churchill put it best in a speech given on November 10th: "Now this is not the end, it is not even the beginning of the end. But it is perhaps the end of the beginning."

On March 9th, 1943, Rommel left Africa for the last time. Hitler had decided that "he had become a pessimist" and ordered him home on sick leave.[114] In fine Nazi propagandist form, Rommel's exit from Africa was kept secret, so that the "Rommel Effect" would continue to intimidate the Allied forces.[115]

Chapter 9: Northwest Europe

By May, Rommel had met with both Goebbels and Hitler to discuss his next assignment. The Germans, including Rommel, feared that an allied invasion of Sicily and the Italian mainland would result in a quick Italian surrender, leaving Germany open to attack. Rommel was to prepare a plan to occupy Italy in such a case. When the invasion came in July, however, Hitler was convinced that Mussolini would stand against the allies, and insisted on concentrating on the eastern front.[116] By September, the Italians had signed an armistice with the allied forces that had invaded the mainland, and on the 8th, Hitler had put Operation Axis into motion, with Rommel in charge.[117] Only a week later he was hospitalized with appendicitis, requiring both surgery and a ten-day recovery. Rommel's concerns for his family's safety grew in the face of the war's outlook. He instructed Lucie to begin looking for a new home in northern Germany to avoid the bombing raids he anticipated would soon be launched from Italy. Rommel continued to be viewed as a pessimist by the Nazi leadership, including Hitler. Though he recommended that Germany attempt to hold their lines 90 miles north of Rome, his rival for supreme commander, Kesselring, advocated the line be placed 90 miles south of the city. As Rommel offered the Nazi leadership realistic views on what the German armies were capable of, he was pushed more and more to the outside Hitler's circle of influence.[118]

---

[114] Ibid., 180.
[115] Ibid., 181.
[116] Ibid., 196-203.
[117] Ibid., 223.
[118] Ibid., 228.

Only nine weeks after Hitler brought Rommel home from North Africa, his replacement, Colonel General Juergen von Arnim, was forced to surrender to the Allies. As Rommel had predicted, Africa was, at this point, unwinnable for the Germans. Over 100,000 German soldiers were taken as prisoners of war, and Italy, now open to invasion, would fall in 1943.[119] Historian Samuel Mitcham Jr. claims that Hitler told Rommel he had made a mistake, and "should have listened."[120]

In August, 1943, Rommel was called out of what could be considered a disgraced retirement in the "Fuhrer Reserve," and sent to Italy to attempt to maintain control of the north. After a disagreement with Kesselring about the portion of Italy they would be able to hold, Rommel was removed from Italy as well.[121]

By mid-1943, Hitler's Atlantic Wall looked formidable, with trenches, ditches, machine-gun nests, minefields, fortified artillery placements and bunkers. Over 8,000 such installations were operational, and 2,300 anti-tank guns and 2,700 guns larger than 75 mm were in place. However, Field-Marshall Gerd von Rundstedt, commander of the German forces in France, was still less than convinced of the strength of the Atlantic wall. He, along with many commanders in France, felt that the notion of an impenetrable Atlantic Wall was more of a figment of Hitler's imagination than a reality on the ground. Von Rundstedt argued that a static line defense such as the Atlantic Wall was only of use if there was defensible depth in the form of fall-back positions.

---

[119] Samuel W. Mitcham, Jr., *The Desert Fox in Normandy: Rommel's Defense of Fortress Europe* (Westport, CT: Praeger Publishers, 1997), 2.
[120] Ibid.
[121] Ibid.

Field Marshal Gerd von Rundstedt

A picture of German fortifications on D-Day. The countless small holes show the extent, and limited effect, of Allied shelling.

Hitler, at the behest of von Rundstedt to reinforce France, sent Rommel to the area to shore up German defenses. Finally, as Hitler anticipated an Allied invasion in 1944, he asked Rommel to inspect the Atlantic Wall, in what Young calls "a fake, a paper hoop for the allies to jump through."[122] No wonder Rommel was "appalled" as he moved from Denmark into France to make a report on Germany's lauded defenses. Young lists the deficiencies Rommel discovered in his inspection tour: army artillery with no cover, lack of concrete shelters at the strongholds, lack of minefields for defense, and a general lack of coordination between the navy and army defenses.[123] Rommel set to work on addressing the issues, but was not given a position of command until January of 1944, which would prove to be too late to save Germany from the Normandy invasion.

Nevertheless, Rommel oversaw the laying of millions of mines and underwater obstacles on the most likely landing beaches of the region, which was designed to keep the Allies from successfully landing ashore and driving the invasion force back into the sea. He wanted as much defenses as possible on the beaches, with infantry divisions as close as possible to landing sites and panzer divisions nearby to immediately strike at the landing forces.

Even as the Atlantic Wall was strengthened, *Operation Fortitude* tricked Hitler into keeping 13 divisions in Norway rather than reinforcing the Normandy peninsula. It had also tricked German High Command into believing that 89 Allied divisions were preparing to land, with enough landing craft to bring 20 divisions ashore. In actuality, the figures were 47 and 6 respectively.

---

[122] Desmond Young, 207.
[123] Ibid., 207-209.

Overreliance on intelligence crippled German defensive efforts in Normandy; it would not have taken a genius commander to realize that an exhausted Britain and a U.S. Army fighting a multi-theater war in the Pacific, Africa, Western Europe and Italy could not have fielded 87 divisions to attack Europe. Instead the Germans swallowed Allied misinformation hook, line and sinker. Statistics show the extent to which the German High Command was tricked by Allied deception plans. The Fifteenth Army, based at Pas de Calais, grew to a strength of 18 infantry and two panzer divisions. The Seventh Army, based in Normandy, had just 14 infantry and one panzer divisions.

As the Allies landed, Rommel and his generals had misjudged the main landing area, and in part, continued to believe that the D-Day invasion was a feint, rather than the real thing, until it was too late. To make matters more complicated for the smaller force defending Normandy, the size of their theater of operations stretched for 995 miles of coastline. Rommel and von Rundstedt were both reminded of Frederick II's maxim, "He who defends everything, defends nothing."

Chapter 10: The July 20 Plot

There is much controversy surrounding the end of Erwin Rommel's career and life. His expertise as a field marshal proved insufficient to tip the war in favor of Germany and the Axis powers, and as the Allies drove further into Europe, it was evident that the war was coming to an end. The German war effort was slowing, and resources to supply the front lines were becoming more limited. This was a pattern Rommel knew well, as even when he was fighting in Africa he had been pressed to the limit and lacked the necessary resources: "Rommel's German superiors expected much from him, but they would not allocate adequate resources to him. If the Germans had taken Crete and used it to facilitate the flow of increased logistics to Rommel, he would have been able to accomplish much more. It was not Rommel's function, given his position, to control his logistics."[124]

As supply lines failed due to Allied invasion and heavy bombing, opinions changed as to how Germany should handle its obvious and nearing defeat. A conspiracy to assassinate Hitler developed inside the Third Reich, of which it is believed Rommel was a part, or supported in some measure, but accounts of his involvement are limited due to the lack of conspirators that survived.[125] Some have suggested that Rommel believed a negotiated surrender was a more preferable approach to ending the war, and his connection to any assassination plot should be dismissed as conspiratorial hearsay.[126]

Either way, by July of 1944, German high-leadership was in disarray. Hitler dismissed Field

---

[124] Joseph Forbes in "Letters," *Military Review* 78, no. 3 (1998).
[125] Beckett, Ian (2014). "Introduction". *Rommel Reconsidered*. (Mechanicsburg, PA: Stackpole Books), 6.
[126] Naumann, Klaus "Afterword". In Charles Messenger. *Rommel: Leadership Lessons from the Desert Fox*. (Basingstoke, NY: Palgrave Macmillan, 2009), 189-191.

Marshal Gerd von Rundstedt after the Allies successfully took the beaches in Normandy. Hitler suspected that the "defeatism" from which he claimed von Rundstedt suffered had crept into subordinate leadership. When Gunther von Kluge took von Rundstedt's place, he immediately turned his attention to Rommel. Hitler's suspicions were right: Rommel did not see a German victory on the horizon. The information he received from the front lines led him to believe it would only be a matter of time before the Allies broke through German defenses. By this time, Hitler was suspicious of Rommel's allegiances due to reports of his connection to a resistance movement.

Stauffenberg

Count Claus Schenk von Stauffenberg played the central role in Operation Valkyrie, also known as the July 20th bomb plot, the 1944 attempt on Hitler's life that (unlike most of the Army's previous efforts) nearly succeeded. The subject of numerous books and at least one high-profile popular film, Operation Valkyrie came even closer than Georg Elser's bombing attempt to killing Hitler.

Since at least 1943, Stauffenberg had involved himself in covert resistance to Hitler and scheming against the Fuhrer's life. The officers engaged in these ambitious plans worked out a strategy, "Valkyrie," that would enable the seizure of key spots and the arrest or elimination of crucial Nazi personnel in the event Hitler died, allowing the schemers to assume the reins of power or at least attempt to do so.

Stauffenberg received a promotion to the rank of colonel on July 1st, 1944 and found himself participating in meetings at the Berghof as an aide to General Friedrich Fromm. The newly minted colonel answered summons to appear at the Berghof on July 8th, when Fromm consulted with Hitler and other top officers on the conduct of the war. Stauffenberg smuggled a bomb into the conference room but did not detonate it, perhaps due to the absence of Himmler and Goering, whom the resistance consistently earmarked for elimination at the same time as Hitler to increase the chances of Nazi collapse.

Fromm

The plotters now felt extreme urgency in bringing about Hitler's death, and two factors impelled them: fear of Gestapo discovery, and the Allies' advance. The men hoped to gain a negotiated peace with the Allies rather than an unconditional surrender following their slaying of the Fuhrer, but such an outcome remained possible only as long as the Allies remained outside Germany's borders. Hitler must die before the Allies reached German soil or the plan would be in vain.

The inner circle of men at the heart of the plot – Oster, Stauffenberg and his brother, Canaris, Beck, Tresckow, Schlabrendorff, Witzleben, and other longtime resisters, along with new faces such as Hans-Ulrich von Oertzen, remained conflicted about the plan but determined to proceed despite their personal shame at "betraying" German military obedience. Stauffenberg explained his thoughts several days before the July 20th bombing attempt. While his brother, Berthold von Stauffenberg, judged the attempt foredoomed but declared the necessity of trying in any case. Claus von Stauffenberg remarked, "It is now time that something was done. But he who has the courage to do something must do so in the knowledge that he will go down in German history as a traitor. If he does not do it, however, he will be a traitor to his conscience." (Hoffmann, 1996, 374).

Stauffenberg sought another opportunity to blow up Hitler on July 11th, again at the Berghof. Though he successfully smuggled a bomb into the conference room, Stieff – now in on the plan – dissuaded him from throwing it due to Himmler's absence. It's also possible his courage failed him or he could not bear the stain on his military honor.

On July 14th, Hitler moved his headquarters from the Berghof to the Wolfsschanze ("Wolf's Lair") in Prussia, a massive forest complex near Rastenburg. Stauffenberg accompanied the staff, still carrying his briefcase bomb, and on July 15th, he placed the briefcase in the Wolfsschanze's conference room and left. Before the bomb exploded, however, Stieff entered the room, removed the briefcase, and disarmed the timing mechanism, once again possibly saving Hitler's life.

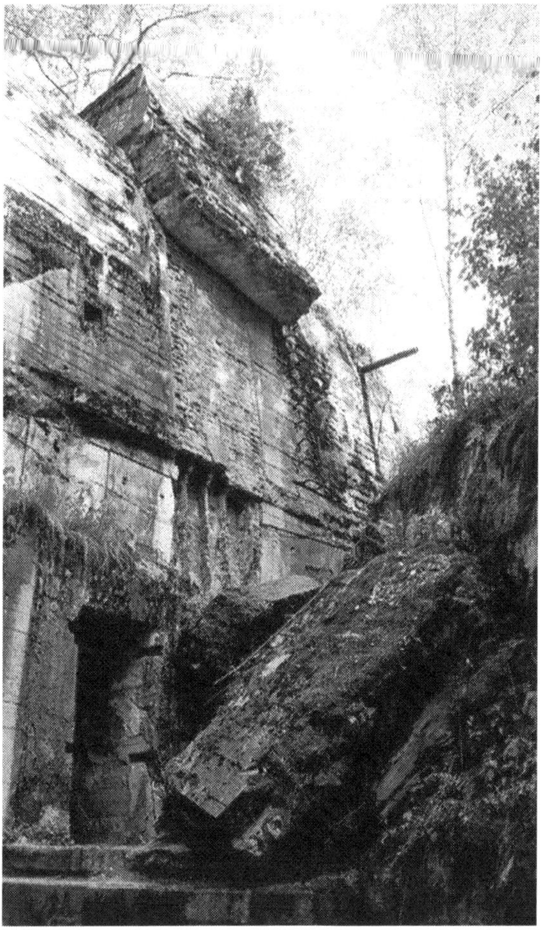

Pictures taken at the Wolf's Lair

Stauffenberg (standing on the far left) next to Hitler on July 15, 1944

On July 19th, dozens of officers prepared for the seizure of key points in Berlin and elsewhere on the following day, along with the broadcast of messages announcing Hitler's death and the end of the Third Reich. Few expected success, least of all Stauffenberg, but all stood ready to carry out their part in the unfolding drama.

Stauffenberg arrived at Rastenburg airport at 10:00 a.m. on July 20th carrying an innocuous briefcase. Meeting fellow conspirator Werner von Haeften shortly before the 12:30 p.m. military conference with Hitler, he gave Haeften the empty briefcase and received the explosive briefcase, containing two bombs, in its place. Stauffenberg armed the first bomb but then found himself interrupted by an urgent telephone call. Apparently slightly panicked, he left the second bomb behind, halving the explosive power of the briefcase and, most likely, accidentally saving

Hitler's life.

When the meeting in the Wolfsschanze's map room with its gigantic oak table finally got underway, Stauffenberg entered and put the explosive briefcase down just three feet from where Hitler stood, behind one of the oak table's massive legs. He then left again, blending in with the aides who hurried in and out, fetching papers, making telephone calls, sending telegraph messages, and the like. At 12:42 p.m., the bomb exploded, as one of the 40 men present later recalled: "In a flash the map room became a scene of stampede and destruction… there was nothing but wounded men groaning, the acrid smell of burning and charred fragments of maps and papers fluttering in the wind." (Moorhouse, 2006, 190).

Many of those present died, and most of the rest suffered wounds, but thanks to the protection offered by the table leg and the table itself, Hitler survived with minor injuries except for perforations in his eardrums. The blast had blown his pants right off of him.

A picture of the damage done by the bomb

The explosion attracted little attention for several minutes, muffled by the walls and unremarkable in a location where frequent weapons drills occurred. One soldier even remarked to Stauffenberg as the would-be assassin hurried out to his car that the explosion likely marked the death of a forest animal incautiously straying into the Wolfsschanze's minefields. Stauffenberg stayed only long enough to see a corpse wrapped in Hitler's cloak carried out of the map room. Failing to check the cadaver's identity, he assumed the Fuhrer lay dead under the blood-soaked cloth and thus left for Rastenburg airport, where, despite the alarm raised by the time he arrived, he managed to bully an air crew into releasing an aircraft for an immediate flight to Berlin.

Stauffenberg's co-conspirator at the Wolfsschanze, Fellgiebel, soon learned that Hitler had survived and telephoned the officers in Berlin. His spoke so vaguely, however, that the men had little idea what had happened or failed to happen at the Wolf's Lair. Finally, at around 3:15 p.m., they decided to launch the coup attempt despite the near certainty Hitler remained alive.

For a few hours, things appeared to go the conspirators' way. The Valkyrie troops mobilized and seized a number of key objectives by 6:00 p.m. However, at around this time, Hitler began calling officers he knew, enabling them to recognize his voice and realize he was still alive, and many of the officers soon began standing their troops down. Even Witzleben called off his soldiers and went home by 9:00 p.m. Hitler seemed euphoric at his survival, laughing and joking with the other people at the Wolfsschanze and declaring loudly, over and over again, "I am invulnerable, I am immortal!"

In the meantime, General Fromm, Stauffenberg's immediate superior, took Stauffenberg and other conspirators prisoner, just as they had taken him prisoner a few hours before. Beck attempted to kill himself but failed, leaving him writhing on the floor in agony until Fromm ordered a sergeant to mercifully shoot him.

Stauffenberg and a number of other conspirators met a swift fate at the hands of Fromm's men, who dragged them from the building. "In the courtyard outside, several military vehicles pulled up, their headlights glaring. [...] In the middle stood an execution squad consisting of Lieutenant Werner Schady and ten noncommissioned officers. [...] Olbricht was the first to be shot. Next it was Stauffenberg's turn, but just as the squad fired, Haeften, in a defiant gesture, threw himself into the hail of bullets. When the squad again took aim at Stauffenberg, he shouted, 'Long live sacred Germany.' Before the sound of his voice died away, shots resounded." (Fest, 1994, 172). Himmler ordered Fromm's arrest shortly thereafter, suspecting him due to the great haste with which he killed Stauffenberg.

A wave of arrests followed in Germany and France as Gestapo interrogations, captured documents, and the actions of conspirators revealed those who participated in the scheme. Some of the men involved successfully committed suicide before their capture. Tresckow, a longtime plotter against the Fuhrer's life, managed to kill himself on the Eastern Front before the Gestapo or SS arrested him, and indeed before they even suspected him. He arranged to drive out alone with a submachine gun, which he fired, then detonated a grenade against his body to simulate his killing by partisans. Another plotter, Hans-Ulrich von Oertzen, asked to urinate while being arrested. The Gestapo allowed him to use the bathroom in his office, where he thrust a live grenade into his mouth and blew his own head off.

Many, however, fell alive into Gestapo hands and suffered extensive torture as the secret police worked to extract more names and more details from their captives. Beatings, electric shocks, the medieval rack, and a special finger-piercing device were all used during the interrogations. Some displayed their injuries in court, causing consternation in a society not entirely accustomed to the excesses of a dictatorial regime even after 11 years of rule by Adolf Hitler.

Eventually, the People's Court, headed by the notorious, intelligent, and corrupt Roland Freisler, tried dozens of prisoners and condemned them to death. 7,000 arrests led to no less than 4,980 executions, including some which amounted to no more than personal revenge by SS personnel against people they hated. Fromm died before a firing squad, and the court convicted Arthur Nebe, the Kripo head, sentencing him to hang.

Freisler

The Court's sessions continued for months, but on February 3rd, 1945, a massive Allied air raid struck Berlin while the court was in session. Freisler, a courageous man despite his other failings, returned from the air raid cellars to fetch certain important documents from the courtroom. A bomb struck the People's Court, collapsing part of the building and causing a falling beam to fatally strike Freisler on the head.

Imprisonment in Plotzensee constituted a form of torture in itself. Each prisoner occupied a tiny cell, continually illuminated by a bare electric bulb. The guards shackled each man to the wall with chains permitting him to reach the bed and toilet, but no more. Most prisoners lived in total isolation except when brought out for interrogation, torture, trial, or execution. The prison diet consisted of bread, plus soup made from potato peelings and gristle. The warders provided no exercise time and many men never saw the outdoors or the sky again, immured in fear-drenched boredom for months until the guards came to drag them to the execution chamber. Many of the condemned Valkyrie plotters suffered the penalty of hanging underneath a sturdy beam placed in a large, bare room with two tall, arched windows in Plotzensee Prison. The room still exists, and the beam still stands in the chamber as a memorial. The Gestapo equipped the beam with five large steel hooks to which they attached hemp nooses.

The Gestapo hanged the final group of 28 July 20th "traitors" on April 20th, 1945 as a birthday present to the Fuhrer. Many of the victims made no effort to either kill themselves or escape prior to their arrest, preferring to await the Gestapo with "dignity" and thus express their belief they were neither criminals nor traitors but brave German officers doing their duty and accepting the consequences of failure. Peter Yorck von Wartenburg wrote to his wife during the trials, "I, too, am dying for my country, and even if it seems to all appearances a very inglorious and disgraceful death, I shall hold up my head and I only hope that you will not believe this to be from pride or delusion. We wished to light the torch of life and now we stand in a sea of flames." (Thomsett, 1997, 236).

By then, Rommel had been dead for months, the result of being named by a fellow officer as a conspirator in the failed plot to assassinate Hitler.[127] But the question remains, did Rommel participate in the plot to kill Hitler? It goes without saying that Hitler's determination to continue fighting had forced Rommel to take pause. Rommel, a long time combat veteran now in his second major world war, had seen war up close. He was a determined fighter, but he was not a lunatic. As the shift in power took place in Europe, and Berlin was legitimately within reach of the Allies, Rommel and other German officers were forced to determine where to place their political ties to best insulate themselves after defeat.

Karl Strölin, a long-time Nazi party member and politician, claimed Rommel had been brought into the anti-Hitler conspiracy by three close friends in early 1944:[128] "Reports indicate that both Rommel and General Kluge knew there was an assassination plot in the works, and that

---

[127] James P. Duffy and Vincent L. Ricci, *Target Hitler: The Plots to Kill Adolf Hitler* (Westport, CT: Praeger Publishers, 1992), 10.
[128] Shirer, William L. (1960). *The Rise and Fall of the Third Reich.* New York: Simon and Schuster, 1031,1177.

both men agreed to support [the]…interim government once the Fuehrer was dead."[129] What if the plan had failed? What if Hitler could not be stopped? For those who see Rommel and his fellow officers as essentially pragmatists, attempting to reposition themselves as the war drew to an end, "They made it clear that if there was no assassination they would not become involved in the coup. It is incredible that these two men, with hundreds of thousands of combat troops at their command, and who were both resolved that Germany was headed toward a crushing defeat, feared Hitler so much that they refused to do anything to stop the carnage unless he was dead."[130]

The evidence linking Rommel to the resistance is not overwhelming, but there are two specific pieces of information that may indicate his involvement. First, in April of 1945, Rommel's son, Manfred, revealed that his father had been forced to commit suicide. This connection to the similar deaths of conspirators looked suspicious. Secondly, Hans Speidel, a German general and chief of staff for Rommel when he was appointed Field Marshal, claimed that he had discussed directly with Rommel the necessity for Hitler to be assassinated. While Speidel gave no details linking Rommel to the plot, it is at least reasonable to assume Rommel knew about the assassination plot and impending coup.

James Duffy argues that rumors of a plot to kill Hitler were widely known among German generals, and knowledge of this plot does not imply conspiratorial guilt. While there is testimony of Rommel's involvement, it appears to center around his knowledge of the plot, rather than of his direct participation.[131] In and around these theories lie accusations of closed door meetings and secret communications between Rommel and anti-Hitler conspirators, but most of these cannot be substantiated. In a final attempt to clear her husband's name, Lucie Rommel made a public statement which included the following: "I want it made quite clear that my husband had no part whatever in the preparations for, or the execution of, the July 20th plot."[132]

By October of 1944, Hitler's paranoia with respect to Rommel was complete. He had determined Rommel must be removed, and permanently. After the July 20th failed attempt on Hitler's life, many of the military leaders involved took their own lives to save themselves from Hitler's wrath and public "flogging." Rommel knew his name was associated with the plot and he was aware Hitler would be coming after him.

On October 14, 1944, German generals Wilhelm Burgdorf and Ernst Maisel visited Rommel in his home in Herrlingen. Outside, SS troops stood by, having been instructed to kill Rommel if he attempted to escape. Rommel was told that he had been accused of associating with conspirators, and had been implicated in the July 20th assassination plot against Hitler. They gave him the choice to die by his own hand, or face a public trial. Rommel was promised that the Nazis would

---

[129] Duffy and Ricci, 176.
[130] Ibid, 176.
[131] Ibid, 11.
[132] Roger Manvell and Heinrich Fraenkel, *The Men Who Tried to Kill Hitler* (New York: Coward-McCann, 1965), 165.

report his death as an accident, and that his family would be left alone. He would leave with the generals, and on his way to Ulm would drink poison. At the end of the hour-long meeting, Rommel emerged, having chosen to take his own life: "A great change had come over Rommel's expression as he went to his wife and said: 'In a quarter of an hour I shall be dead.' He told her that he had been accused of complicity in the July plot. Hitler, he said, was offering him the choice between taking poison and facing the People's Court. He was not afraid of the Court, but he was convinced that he would never get to Berlin alive. And so he was choosing poison. He bid his wife and son goodbye, exchanged a few words with his ADC, and putting his hand on the man's shoulder, said: 'Aldinger, this is it.'"[133]

A state funeral was prepared. Plans for monuments in Rommel's honor were presented. Every attempt was made to honor Rommel as a hero, "but all attempts to adorn this grave with wreaths, memorials and speeches failed to silence rumors among the people that Rommel had not died a natural death, but had been killed by Hitler."[134]

A picture of the funeral

---

[133] Eberhard Zeller, The Flame of Freedom: The German Struggle against Hitler, trans. R. P. Heller and D. R. Masters (Boulder, CO: Westview Press, 1994), 378.
[134] Ibid., 379.

Rommel was one of Hitler's many generals and those in positions of military leadership executed following the July 20th plot. Between July, 1944, and the end of the war, an estimated 5,000 Germans directly and indirectly connected to the plot were arrested and executed alongside Rommel for crimes against the Nazi party.[135]

Ironically, at Rommel's funeral, the traditional German march for honoring fallen soldiers was played:
I had a buddy,
you could never find a better one.
The drum rolled for battle,
he walked by my side
at the same speed in step.
A bullet came flying--
for me or for you?
It tore him away,
he lay at my feet
like a piece of myself.
He stretched out his hand to me
while I was reloading.
I can't give you my hand--
stay there in eternal life,
my good buddy!

Chapter 11: The Rommel Myth

While it is true that historians, especially in recent times, have revisited the people and events of the past for the purpose of re-examination, the intensity with which Erwin Rommel's reputation has been scrutinized is marked. One of his biographers, Desmond Young, whose book, *Rommel: The Desert Fox*, is considered the most acclaimed work on the general, has been accused by some of attempting an "Anglophone rehabilitation"[136] of Rommel, specifically called out as constructing a fiction, since "the real Erwin Rommel was not the same man that Desmond Young created back in 1950."[137]

The idea of "the Rommel Myth" has been perpetuated by many modern scholars, and the debates over his real merits as a military general, as a strategist, and as a person continue. Alaric Searle, director of the Center for European Military Security at the University of Salford, argues that the British perpetuated the Rommel Myth to excuse their own, poor performance in North

---

[135] Ibid., 379-380.
[136] Mark Connelly in *Rommel: A Reappraisal*. Ed. Ian Becektt. (South Yorkshire, Great Britain: Pen and Sword, 2013). 162.
[137] Alaric Searle in *Rommel: A Reappraisal*. Ed. Ian Becket. (South Yorkshire, Great Britain: Pen and Sword, 2013). 26.

Africa. By making the general a brilliant strategist and a miracle worker of sorts when it came to inspiring his own men, the British public could more easily accept British losses.[138] One problem stood in the way of Rommel's rehabilitation—his allegiance to Hitler and the Nazi party. For those who believe that Rommel's reputation is merely myth, Rommel's relationship with Hitler and his personal disdain for the actions of the Nazis have been fabricated, or at the very least exaggerated to allow the myth greater credibility.

Beyond the simple desire to excuse the performance of the British troops, revisionists argue, lies a far more significant reason for the creation of the Rommel Myth. After World War II ended and the Soviet Union began to challenge the west in Europe, the British, Americans, and the French were in a difficult position. West Germany was still needed to help form a geographical point of resistance against the spread of communism in Europe, and for this, a German rearmament would have to take place. Searle and others claim that developing a legendary German general who was palatable and talented, and perhaps even a good and honorable man who had desired to assassinate Hitler, would go far in convincing the Western public that their former Soviet ally now was the enemy, while the Germans were friends.[139] Basil Liddell Hart, a British journalist, and Desmond Young, are the two main writers whose works are accused of having propelled the Rommel Myth.[140] Searle has written critically and extensively on the motives and scholarship of Hart, who he claims was a failed journalist and writer looking to rehabilitate his reputation at the conclusion of World War II. "Here was a potentially malleable group of individuals who could help him re-establish his reputation as a military authority," Searle writes of a group of German generals housed in an English jail with whom Hart had made contact.[141]

No matter what one's final assessment on Rommel's abilities and intent is, it remains an undeniable fact that his name is highly and unusually recognized by the general public. Daniel Allen Butler witnessed this while penning Rommel's biography. He found people from California, Minnesota, and Florida, to Canada and Northern Ireland,[142] who would "blurt out 'Rommel!'" in answer to his request to name a World War II general.

As Rommel wrote in *Infantry Attacks*, "Winning the men's confidence requires much of a commander. He must exercise care and caution, look after his men, live under the same hardships, and—above all— apply self-discipline. But once he has their confidence, his men will follow him through hell and high water."

Those who "follow Rommel," whether they are the cadets he influenced, the men he led into

---

[138] Ibid., 7-8.
[139] Ibid., 8.
[140] Ibid., 9.
[141] Alaric Searle, "A Very Special Relationship: Basil Liddell Hart, Wehrmacht Generals and the Debate on West German Rearmament, 1945-1953," *War in History* 5, no. 3 (1998): Accessed July 26, 2016, doi:10.1177/096834459800500304.
[142] Daniel Allen Butler, 10.

battle, or the military buffs who make up his modern-day admirers, could be said to have their confidence in a man without pedigree, but with plenty of determination and a sense of honor. It will continue to be left to the students of history to pass judgment on the life of a man whose talents and ambitions ended tragically, at the hands of those who had most benefitted from them.

Online Resources

Other World War II titles by Charles River Editors

Other titles about Nazi Germany by Charles River Editors

Other titles about Rommel on Amazon

Bibliography

Barnett, Correlli. *The Desert Generals*. New York: Viking Press, 1961.

Battistelli, Pier Paolo Erwin. *Rommel: Leadership, Strategy, Conflict*. New York: Bloomsbury Publishing, 2012.

Beckett, Ian F. *Rommel: A Reappraisal*. South Yorkshire, Great Britain: Pen and Sword, 2013.

Brighton, Terry Patton. *Montgomery, and Rommel: Masters of War*. New York: Crown Publishers, 2008.

Butler, Daniel Allen. *Field Marshall: The Life and Death of Erwin Rommel*. Philadelphia: Casemate Publishers, 2015.

Connelly, Mark. In *Rommel: A Reappraisal*. Ed. Ian Beckett. South Yorkshire, Great Britain: Pen and Sword, 2013.

Duffy, James P. and Ricci, Vincent L. *Target Hitler: The Plots to Kill Adolf Hitler*. Westport, CT: Praeger Publishers, 1992.

Flint, Hannah. "Revealed: Desert Fox Erwin Rommel was given his legendary goggles by a British POW in return for retrieving a stolen hat." *The UK Daily Mail Online*. April 20, 2015. Accessed August 6, 2016.

Forbes, Joseph. "Letters," *Military Review 78*, no. 3. 1998.

Fraenkel, Heinrich and Manvell, Roger. *Goering: The Rise and Fall of the Notorious Nazi Leader*. London: frontline Books, 2011.

Fraser, David. *Knight's Cross: A Life of Field Marshal Erwin Rommel*. New York: HarperCollins. 1993.

Hoffmann, Karl. "Erwin Rommel, 1891-1944." Commanders in Focus. London: Brassey's. 2004.

Kater, Michael H. *Hitler Youth*. Cambridge, MA: Harvard University Press, 2004.

Manvell, Roger and Fraenkel, Heinrich. *The Men Who Tried to Kill Hitler*. New York: Coward-McCann, 1965.

Miller, Frank J. "The Ancient Classics: Some Notes on Classical Training in a German Gymnasium." *The School Review*, Vol. 12, No. 1 (Jan., 1904), pp. 97-108. The University of Chicago Press.

Mitcham, Jr., Samuel W. *The Desert Fox in Normandy: Rommel's Defense of Fortress Europe*. Westport, CT: Praeger Publishers, 1997.

Mitcham, Jr., Samuel W. *Rommel's Greatest Victory: The Desert Fox and the Fall of Tobruk, Spring 1942*. Novato, CA: Presidio Press, 1998.

Mitcham Jr., Samuel W. *Triumphant Fox: Erwin Rommel and the Rise of the Afrika Korps*. Mechanicsburg, Pennsylvania: Stackpole Books, 1984.

Naumann, Klaus "Afterword". In Charles Messenger. *Rommel: Leadership Lessons from the Desert Fox.* Basingstoke, NY: Palgrave Macmillan, 2009.

Ridge, George. "The White War: Life and Death on the Italian Front 1915-1919," *Military Review* 89, no. 6 (2009).

Rommel, Erwin. *Infantry Attacks*. Barnsley: South Yorkshire: Greenhill Books, 1990.

Searle, Alaric. "A Very Special Relationship: Basil Liddell Hart, Wehrmacht Generals and the Debate on West German Rearmament, 1945-1953," *War in History* 5, no. 3 (1998): Accessed July 26, 2016, doi:10.1177/096834459800500304.

Searle, Alaric. In *Rommel: A Reappraisal*. Ed. Ian Becket. South Yorkshire, Great Britain: Pen and Sword, 2013.

Shirer, William L. *The Rise and Fall of the Third Reich*. New York: Simon and Schuster, 1960.

Stern, Fritz. *The Politics of Cultural Despair: A Study in the Rise of the Germanic Ideology*. Berkeley: University of California Press, 1974.

Varangis, Nicholas "Rommel's Ghost Division." *Warfare History Network*: World War II. June 1, 2016.

Wette, Wolfram. *The Wehrmacht.* Boston: Harvard University Press, 2009.

Young, Desmond. *Rommel: The Desert Fox*. London, Fontana Books, 1950.

Zeller, Eberhard. *The Flame of Freedom: The German Struggle against Hitler,* trans. R. P. Heller and D. R. Masters. Boulder, CO: Westview Press, 1994.

Free Books by Charles River Editors

We have brand new titles available for free most days of the week. To see which of our titles are currently free, click on this link.

Printed in Great Britain
by Amazon

Discounted Books by Charles River Editors

We have titles at a discount price of just 99 cents everyday. To see which of our titles are currently 99 cents, [click on this link](#).